ENOUGH!

ENOUGH!

The Revolt
of the American Consumer

DORIS FABER

Farrar, Straus and Giroux · New York

Copyright © 1972 by Doris Faber
All rights reserved
First printing, 1972
Library of Congress catalog card number: 72-81486
ISBN 0-374-32193-0
Printed in the United States of America
Published simultaneously in Canada by Doubleday Canada Ltd., Toronto
Designed by Cynthia Basil

Contents

ENOUGH!

1

Blowing the Whistle

Who broke the code?

In a small office less than a mile from the White House, a woman smiles. It was not really too difficult, she remarks, and she picks up a pencil.

19033. Quickly writing these numbers, she explains that they mean the item under investigation is part of lot number one, manufactured on the thirty-third day of 1969. For the trick is to draw the right circles, and so saying she draws three circles—the first around the first digit on her pad, the second around the second, the third around the last three. "Lot number, year, day of the year," she identifies each circle briskly.

The woman speaking is the director of the Consumer Federation of America and she is describing the start of a new drive by her agency. The aim of this particular program is to protect the nation's babies from stale or even spoiled canned infant formula.

• • •

In a shabby neighborhood near Shea Stadium, grand-mothers are leaning out of windows, straining to see what is causing such commotion down on the street. There are vans parked along the curb, and television crews are

3

tripping over each other's equipment. In the center of the disturbance, seemingly unperturbed, a former Miss America emerges from a meat market. "We're out to stop crime in the shops!" she exclaims into a battery of microphones.

She is Bess Myerson, New York City's Commissioner of Consumer Affairs, and she is conducting one of her raids on merchants suspected of cheating the public. Her target for today is illegal hamburger—ground meat mixed with too much fat or cereal or some other substance masquerading as beef. "Shamburgers!" she says. "You wouldn't believe some of the selling practices that go on in this city."

• • •

In Los Angeles, a telephone rings. A young man with a large moustache, who has recently joined what he likes to call "the fraud squad," picks up the receiver. He listens, jots down some notes, promises to report back soon. "Another swimming-pool complaint," he explains.

In the official language used by government agencies, he is a consumer-protection specialist, and at this particular regional headquarters of the Federal Trade Commission, he often handles complaints about misleading advertising and poor workmanship on the part of some builders of swimming pools.

• • •

In Minneapolis, a reporter for the *Star* finds a letter from a distressed grandfather in her morning mail. In it he says that after he bought a stuffed Easter rabbit to give his granddaughter, he was horrified to discover sharp pins sticking out of its ears. The reporter investigates, and the next day's newspaper has a story headlined:

THIS BUNNY IS NOT FUNNY FOR LITTLE HONEY

As a result, the chain store that sold the dangerous rabbit protests to the company that made the toy. The manufacturer says the pins were used to hold the ears in place while glue was applied. The pins were supposed to have been removed as soon as the glue dried. The toymaker promises to be more careful in the future.

• • •

On the campus of the University of Tennessee in Knoxville, the assorted problems involved in publicizing consumer grievances are aired at a special three-day workshop under the auspices of the Southern Newspaper Publishers Association.

• • •

In a junior high school in Indiana, a teacher who has recently attended a special training course in consumer education gives her class the following assignment to work on over the weekend:

Tom has just made the school football team. In order to practice at home, he had to buy his own football. After the football was used twice, the seams began to split and the football became deflated. What should Tom do?

If he does return it to the store, what proof does he have that he purchased the football from that particular store?

What should Tom have done before making the purchase that would have been helpful?

• • •

Alerted by a warning from the Food and Drug Administration in Washington, D.C., the Oregon Department of Agriculture sends inspectors to remove a particular brand of candy "love beads" from store shelves throughout the state. Tests have shown that this candy contains enough cadmium to cause illness.

• • •

In San Francisco, most of the leading milk companies agree to adopt a simplified dating system for their containers after a consumer lawsuit is filed contending that the current system is "unfair and deceptive" because it makes it difficult for buyers to find out easily whether the milk in their markets is fresh.

• • •

Selling high fashion is the main business of a department store with branches in many parts of the country. A wealthy-looking, silver-haired woman emerges from an elevator onto an upper floor of the branch store on New York's Fifth Avenue. Under one arm, she carries a large box.

The man at the reception desk stands up to greet her. He is the guardian of what is known here as the Customer Service Bureau—the complaint department in less elegant establishments. "Is yours a *mammoth* problem?" he asks smoothly.

The woman does not seem impressed by his charm. Unwrapping her parcel, she takes out a white purse marred with ugly smudges. "I paid thirty dollars for this," she says. "Less than a month ago. I have used it only twice, and I have just been informed that these stains cannot be removed. I would like my money back."

"But, madam, that purse is suède," the man murmurs. "It is, ah, somewhat perishable. You should not have purchased it if you wished something more sturdy."

"You should not have sold it if it is so useless." The woman frowns at him impatiently. "Will you please return my money?"

He sighs. "No," he says.

The woman's eyes blaze. "This is an outrage!" she cries. "I ought to report you to Nader. Do you want Nader's Raiders to get after you?"

•   •   •

In Washington, D.C., a committee of the United States Senate is holding a hearing on the issue of auto safety. A tall and rumpled-looking man in his late thirties leans forward in the witness chair, making one point after another. Scarcely stopping to glance at the pile of papers on the table in front of him, he seems thoroughly at ease as he tells the lawmakers where their duty lies. His name is Ralph Nader.

"Who does he think he is?" Since the mid-1960's, angry businessmen have been asking the question. Nader holds no public office, he has not been hired to represent any client, yet he has taken it upon himself to keep up a constant attack against some of the country's most powerful industries. On this particular day, he has appeared with folders full of fresh ammunition to fire at auto manufacturers.

Bumpers, fenders, doors—he goes down his list, giving detailed data about the costs to repair these component parts of any model car. He says his figures show that "coldly and with slide-rule precision" the auto industry has been producing cars that cannot be repaired except at exorbitant expense. He accuses the industry of doing this purposely to create a multibillion-dollar replacement market "marked by enormous and monopolistic company markups" on parts. He says the nation's auto-makers are guilty of "massive thievery" that could and should be stopped by act of Congress.

These words provoke a sudden outburst from a committee member.

"You look for the worst in people and not at what's good that's happening in this country," Senator Theodore F. Stevens of Alaska shouts. Pounding his desk to give his point more emphasis, he adds, "You're not giving credit to American industry."

Now Nader's temper flares.

"Do you give credit to a burglar because he doesn't burglarize 90 per cent of the time?" he snaps back.

Within a few hours, this heated exchange is being replayed on television sets in millions of homes all across the United States. The scene requires no sound effects over and above the angry voices of the two disputants, but an imaginative producer might have supplied an extra touch by introducing it with several shrill blasts from a whistle. For, to Nader himself, his role is clear.

He "blows the whistle" whenever he finds people being victimized.

Enough! Stop in the public interest!

This is the basic theme of all his varied campaigns, he thoughtfully tells an interviewer. And his whistle-blowing has been helping to bring about some remarkable changes in all aspects of American life. In cities and towns, among private citizens and elected officials, a new awareness of the need to safeguard the public interest has been growing steadily. This has brought such widespread action on so many different fronts during recent years that a way of describing the phenomenon had to be found. Governor Nelson Rockefeller of New York suggested one—the Consumer Revolution.

Nobody doubts that Ralph Nader has played a leading part in this revolution. Even those—like Senator Stevens—who sincerely feel that Nader has done more harm than good would not deny he has had a tremendous impact. Those who admire Nader give him credit for inspiring one of the most hopeful movements of recent times.

Yet the revolution which he unofficially leads has its roots solidly in the American past. How did it really start? What gave it momentum, then stalled it, and finally made it erupt again? To answer these questions, there is good reason for going back to meet the first successful whistle-blower on the American scene.

2

The Poison Squad

In the spring of 1883, an alert-looking man with an impressive black beard arrived at an old red brick building near the Smithsonian Institution. He was Dr. Harvey W. Wiley from Indiana and he had come to take up his new duties as the head of the chemistry division of the United States Department of Agriculture.

Anybody who knew only the facts about Dr. Wiley's background might have felt that the high point of a typical American success story had now been reached. He had been born in a log cabin, on October 18, 1844, had worked his way through several Hoosier schools, and then Harvard. After winning some small fame as a professor, he had now been offered a government post paying the respectable salary of $2,500 a year.

His future seemed assured. Unless he decided to involve himself in politics, he could look forward to spending the rest of his career quietly supervising experiments in his basement laboratory. But anybody who really knew Dr. Wiley had good reason for doubting whether such a calm prospect would appeal to him.

The circumstances surrounding his acceptance of this post gave Washington a clue as to what to expect. Over six feet in height and weighing about 215 pounds, Dr. Wiley engaged in a constant battle to prevent stoutness from overtaking him. He exercised energetically. Whenever he saw a group of his students tossing a ball around, he hurried out to join them. He even bought one of the first bicycles ever seen in the town of Lafayette, where he was teaching.

His bicycle had a high front wheel and a small back wheel. He bought a pair of knee breeches so he wouldn't risk getting his trousers caught in the machine's spokes. So dressed, Professor Wiley rode daily to conduct his classes at Purdue University. Pedaling down the street from his lodgings, then over a bridge across the Wabash River and on up to the campus, the professor frightened a few horses nearly every day. He must have frightened some university officials too, because one morning he was summoned to appear before a meeting of the institution's board of trustees.

Since he had a medical degree as well as advanced training in the new specialty of chemistry, Dr. Wiley hoped he was going to be offered a salary increase. He had no wife to support, and his struggles to pay for his own schooling had taught him to be careful about money, but he was still finding it necessary to supplement his income from the university by working after hours for the Indiana State Board of Agriculture. If he could have concentrated on teaching and used his spare time to carry out some research projects, he would have been happier.

But as soon as he entered the trustees' meeting room, he could see that the men there were in no mood to give him a raise. Finally a trustee named Mr. Dobblebower spoke up.

"The disagreeable duty has been assigned to me to tell Professor Wiley the cause of his appearance before us," he said. "We have been greatly pleased by the excellence of his instruction and are pleased with the popularity he enjoys among his pupils. We are deeply grieved, however, at his conduct.

"He has put on a uniform and played baseball with the boys, much to the discredit of the dignity of a professor. But the most grave offense of all has lately come to our attention. Professor Wiley has bought a bicycle. Imagine my feelings, and those of other members of the board, on seeing one of our professors dressed up like a monkey and astride a cart-wheel riding along our streets."

Dr. Wiley did not hesitate. "Gentlemen," he said, "I am extremely sorry my conduct has met with your disapproval. I desire to relieve you of all embarrassment on these points. If you will give me a pen and paper, I shall do so."

On being handed these writing materials, he quickly wrote a letter resigning from the university faculty, gave it to Mr. Dobblebower, and left the room.

The next day a reply from the trustees was delivered to him, telling him they had voted unanimously not to accept his resignation. Nevertheless, Dr. Wiley refused to stay. Much as he liked teaching, he suddenly saw this foolish episode as an omen. Ever since his boyhood, he had dreamed of achieving something notable in the service of humanity. How could he do so in such a narrow-minded community?

Fortunately, he was soon given the opportunity to work in the nation's capital and he eagerly accepted it. From his own experience in studying chemistry at Harvard, and also in Germany, Dr. Wiley was convinced that this branch of science stood on the brink of an exciting new era. New techniques for analyzing the precise chemical composition of complex substances were being developed. New testing devices were being perfected. In Berlin, he had been struck by the possibilities for using a sensitive new instrument called a polariscope to learn more about such common substances as sugar. He had brought one back with him and felt sure he would be able to put it to good use at the Department of Agriculture.

During his first years in Washington, that was exactly what he did. Like most of his fellow Americans then, Dr. Wiley had a particular fondness for sugar in practically any form. Prodigious quantities of pies and cakes and candy were being consumed in the United States and, despite efforts to grow sugar cane profitably in Louisiana, most of this sweetening had to be imported from other countries. Why couldn't American farmers produce some acceptable substitute? Dr. Wiley set out enthusiastically to try to find the answer.

He tested sugar made from another cane plant, called sorghum, and sugar made from beets. Both of these crops fit the climatic conditions in large areas of the country and could be made to yield palatable sweeteners. Yet there were numerous problems involved in producing the new sugars economically.

While he kept trying to solve these problems, Dr. Wiley still found time to become a popular figure on the Washington social scene. That he was a bachelor did not mean he craved solitude. The main reason for his remaining unmarried, he cheerfully admitted, was that he liked so many women. He also liked standing up in front of an audience to make a speech.

Whether the occasion was a scientific convention or a women's club meeting, Dr. Wiley could be counted on to provoke laughter and applause. "Let me make the sweets of the nation and I don't care who makes the laws," he would tell a group of ladies. "Childhood without candy would be Heaven without harps," he informed his fellow chemists.

But he had his serious side, too, and it was this side that gradually led him to a wider fame.

Back in Indiana, Dr. Wiley's work for the state's agricultural agency had been concerned mostly with fertilizers. The use of chemicals to improve soil fertility was just beginning on a large scale, and some farmers found cause to wonder if the bags they bought actually contained the promised ingredients. As a result, state-sponsored programs were undertaken in many agricultural areas besides Indiana, providing for an impartial chemical analysis of fertilizer samples and setting penalties for misleading labeling.

Soon after he arrived in Washington, Dr. Wiley began to wonder if some similar form of protection was needed by the nation's food buyers.

In this period following the Civil War, remarkable changes were occurring throughout American life. Before the war, most families had produced many of the items they used in daily living—their own food, clothing, and possibly even their own furniture. Whatever goods they did buy were most often purchased from a neighbor who could personally vouch for their quality.

Then with the outbreak of war, thousands of soldiers had to be outfitted with uniforms. Up until that time, it had been generally accepted that people came in such varying sizes and shapes that there was no practical way of producing clothing other than to make individual garments tailored to individual measurements. However, the overnight demand for uniforms set some ingenious tailors to designing patterns which could be adapted for mass production. By the end of the fighting, a new men's clothing industry had been born.

Under somewhat the same pressures, new ways were also discovered to package various foods and to mass-produce other household items. The steady migration of farm families to cities speeded up this trend, as did the rapid development of new manufacturing methods. Within a few decades,

America turned into a nation of consumers. All over the country, people were buying an ever wider range of goods from increasingly large and impersonal suppliers.

Most people failed to note the full significance of these changes because they were happening so swiftly. The science of economics, which inquires into the mysteries of supply and demand, was still in its infancy. Nevertheless, some men and women did start to think about how unwary consumers could be protected from unscrupulous producers and merchants.

A substantial number of cities and towns passed local laws to prevent the sale of spoiled milk or meat in local markets. A few states also tried to put a wider variety of safeguards into effect, but they were hampered by the fact that state laws had little impact on out-of-state business concerns selling products within their borders. In several European countries where industrialization was taking the same course as in the United States, new measures regulating the purity of foods and drugs on a national basis had been adopted as early as the 1870's. However, the climate of public opinion on this side of the Atlantic definitely did not favor any action by the national government that might in any way hamper the freedom of American businessmen.

Still, food had a particular interest for Dr. Wiley on two counts. As a chemist and as a man devoted to the pleasures of eating, he was disturbed by the mere possibility that the quality of American bread or meat or butter might be deteriorating. In addition, he was still seeking a cause worthy of his whole heart. Suppose the cause of pure food was just what he was looking for?

So Dr. Wiley began making regular purchases from shops in several sections of Washington. At first, he confined his efforts to searching for obvious impurities—and he found plenty. Studying an assortment of spices bought from ordinary grocery stores, he found pepper containing dust or rice or cracker crumbs or even charcoal. He found coffee mixed with ground-up acorns, and canned vegetables showing clear traces of dangerous metallic salts or acids.

Soon he began to uncover a more complicated problem. In dried fruits and in sausages, in practically every category of prepared food on store shelves, he isolated traces of one substance or another that had been purposely added by the processor to make the product less likely to develop an unpleasant color, flavor, or odor. Were these additives harmful? Nobody was sure.

Dr. Wiley had no doubts about one point right from the outset. The results of his investigations must be circulated. His initial steps to publicize his findings took the form of dry scientific reports which he sent to the few other specialists who shared his interest. These had little impact on the general public. During the 1890's, though, he changed his tactics and spoke out more plainly.

Blossoming forth as a poet, he wrote a series of verses entitled "What's in It?" Since many of his public-speaking appearances were at banquets where his audience had just finished an elaborate meal, he had no trouble capturing attention when he recited:

> Oh, maybe this bread contains alum and chalk,
>   Or sawdust chopped up very fine . . .
> I wish I could know what is in it.
>
> The wine which you drink never heard of a grape,
>   But of tannin and coal tar is made . . .
> Oh, I wonder, I wonder, what's in it!

Then he would urge people who shared his concern to join in a campaign aimed at getting Congress to pass a new law that would guarantee the purity of all the food on America's dinner tables.

How could anybody be *against* pure food? Dr. Wiley could not understand why his speeches won him enemies as well as admirers. To him, the case for federal action was so clear that no intelligent person could fail to favor it. Yet spokesmen for many special interests saw the matter in an entirely different light. According to most food processors, for instance, Dr. Wiley was trying to interfere with the freedom of businessmen who had every right to conduct their own business as they thought best. They charged that for reasons known only to himself he wanted to increase the nation's food bills, for that would be the inevitable effect of adopting any play for government regulation of the food industry.

Nonsense, Dr. Wiley retorted. If people wanted a cheap glucose syrup made of cornstarch on their pancakes, instead of natural maple syrup, they should certainly be able to buy it—but they should also be able to learn from the label on the jar exactly what they were buying. "It is not for me to tell my neighbor what he shall eat, what he shall drink, what his religion shall be, or what his politics," said Dr. Wiley. "These are matters which I think every man should be left to settle for himself. Anything in the world I may be pleased to do I want the privilege of doing, even if it is eating limburger cheese."

His joking delighted his friends and distressed his enemies, but it was his "poison squad" that made him famous.

In 1902, after nearly twenty years of trying to advance the cause of pure food without much help from the general public or from his superiors in the Department of Agriculture, Dr. Wiley began a new set of experiments. Scientific data about the real effect of various food preservatives on the human body had never been gathered, so he decided to conduct tests on some volunteers. He set up a special kitchen and dining room adjoining his laboratory, and recruited a dozen healthy young men from among his fellow workers. The plan was to feed them unadulterated food for fifteen days, carefully observing their weight and physical condition after every meal; then to feed them the same diet containing some common preservative, such as borax, for the same length of time, again observing them in every possible way to discover what effect a particular food additive might have on them.

In his own reports about the project, Dr. Wiley avoided high drama. "It appears," he wrote, "that both boric acid and borax, when continuously administered in small doses over a long period, create disturbances of appetite, of digestion, and of health."

The nation's newspapers were far less restrained. Within a few weeks, feature writers had coined their own phrase for the volunteers—the Poison Squad. This captured the imagination of the public, just as another phrase—Nader's Raiders—would captivate the public sixty years later. And just as Ralph Nader's aides would be the focal point of a growing movement, Harvey Wiley's young volunteers provided a sort of symbol for an idea whose time had finally come. Twenty years after embarking on his lonely crusade, Dr. Wiley was no longer alone.

Over the years his feelings about a few subjects other than his work had changed somewhat. For instance, he had shaved off his beard, and had given up bicycling in favor of a "steam buggy" capable of reaching the extreme speed of twenty-five miles per hour. His was the third auto registered in the District of Columbia, but the first in one respect—it was involved in Washington's first recorded collision between a car and a team of horses. Fortunately, the mishap caused no real harm to man, beast, or machine.

But during the months following the establishment of his poison squad, Dr. Wiley had little time for joyriding. Almost every evening, he ate dinner with the group he referred to as his boys, then spent much of the night tabulating test results. On occasion, he even tied an apron around his ample waist and substituted for an ailing cook.

Most of his time, however, was taken up by a seemingly endless series of conferences and meetings. Largely because of his own tireless activities in publicizing the cause, pure food had now become a popular slogan. And as a result of a campaign started by the American Medical Association, which represented the nation's doctors, a similar issue was causing increasing public concern.

At drugstores in every city and town, an ever-growing number of medicines labeled as cures for ailments from tooth-aches to cancer were being sold to anyone willing to pay for them. Some of these preparations proved to be just harmless mixtures of water and flavorings, but others were discovered to be much less innocent. Among the horrible examples discovered by medical researchers were "soothing syrups" for infants found to contain opium. No law forbid such danger-ous mixtures or in any way required manufacturers to sell only remedies that were really effective.

The many people who thought there ought to be a law found their aims were closely allied to those of the pure-food advocates, so the AMA and followers joined forces with them. During the first few years of the new century, these two movements created a rising tide of public opinion favor-ing the passage of a national pure food and drug law.

The General Federation of Women's Clubs, making its first political stand in the name of America's female citizens, flooded Congress with letters urging approval of a bill containing stiff penalties to discourage dishonest manufacturers. The American Medical Association kept making the same demand in the name of the country's 135,000 physicians. Several widely circulated magazines splashed their pages with stories like "The Great American Fraud," listing the actual ingredients found in some so-called cure-all medications.

But at the same time, in public statements and behind the scenes, spokesmen for trade groups were doing their best to discourage Congress from acting. Wholesale druggists said they were already setting up a system of self-policing which would stop any abuses that might have crept into their industry. Vegetable canners and codfish processors insisted that any type of government regulation would violate their Constitutional rights to conduct their own business as they saw fit. Dairymen wanted protection from "unfair competition" by the makers of oleomargarine, but no rules they themselves would have to follow. Representatives of the new margarine industry were against dairy-supported restrictions preventing them from coloring their product an appealing buttery yellow.

In all this confusion of claims that one industry or another deserved some kind of special treatment, even the members of Congress in favor of a new law hesitated. How could any law possibly satisfy so many conflicting interests? Committees of both houses kept holding hearings—and Dr. Wiley and his friends kept doggedly testifying that a new law was badly needed. But one session after another failed to produce any decisive action.

Dr. Wiley could not help but feel increasingly depressed. All he seemed to accomplish was the enlargement of his own reputation among business groups as an instrument of Satan, he wryly told his supporters. Still, he hoped that a reasonable discussion of the issues involved might be helpful and actively sought occasions to speak at business meetings. Arriving in Atlantic City one afternoon to address a convention of vegetable canners, he was met by a man who advised him to board the first train back to Washington. "I am frightened for your safety," the man said.

Dr. Wiley had to stop and think a minute. "Is this a meeting of American citizens?" he finally asked. On being assured that it was, he said briskly that he had never yet been mobbed and he trusted that his fellow Americans would have too much respect for the principle of free speech to provide him with this new experience. So he would stay and deliver his speech as scheduled.

At the meeting, after he was given a rather chilly introduction by the chairman, Dr. Wiley walked forward to begin his talk.

"Is there a man in this audience who would put his hand in his neighbor's pocket, take a dollar from it, and put it in his own pocket? If there is such a person, let him put up his hand."

No hands were raised anywhere in the auditorium.

"Is there a man here," Dr. Wiley went on, "who would so degrade and misbrand a package of his goods as to cheat the consumer out of a dollar of his money when he bought that package? If so, hold up your hand."

Again no hands were raised. But somebody in that hostile audience did an unexpected thing. A sound that was unmistakably applause started at the back of the hall, then spread until the entire assembly appeared to be clapping a sort of apology. After this warming demonstration that the spirit of fair play still survived, despite the bitterness aroused by the pure-food controversy, Dr. Wiley was allowed to deliver the speech he had prepared. He told the canners that their business, and all others, would be better off in the long run with a code of ethics protecting honest merchants as well as consumers from the trickery of the comparatively few dishonest dealers. The proposed pure food and drug law could actually be called a code of business ethics, he said.

While this argument struck Dr. Wiley and some of the audience as unanswerable, there were still a good many businessmen who could not accept it. They felt that no conceivable wording of a law setting up penalties for cheating the public could avoid creating another problem. How were well-meaning dealers who unknowingly sold a worthless or even a harmful product to be protected from being prosecuted as criminals themselves? The only course fair to all concerned was to allow every industry to set its own standards, they insisted.

But why had industry failed to enforce any such standards in the past? How could consumers be sure that new kinds of fraud would not keep popping up in the future? When questions like these were asked, spokesmen for most business groups simply repeated that any interference with the free working of the marketplace was dangerous.

This point of view found ready acceptance among tradition-minded Americans. Although change was in the air—"muckrakers" were at work upsetting many cherished notions about big business—the chance for passage of a pure food and drug law seemed to be fading. Congress was still going through the motions of holding hearings and debating possible revisions, but even Dr. Wiley had lost hope. The bill he had been defending so long was being "completely suffocated," he told his friends.

Then in February of 1906, the whole outlook suddenly

changed. A book by an unknown author—*The Jungle,* by Upton Sinclair—became a runaway best seller.

The story of some poor immigrants from Europe who settled in Chicago, *The Jungle* had been written with a purpose. Sinclair meant his description of the way the newcomers were treated when they sought jobs and homes in "the land of the free" to shock readers into a revolutionary state of mind. His aim was to show how democracy was failing, and to convert his readers to socialism.

Merely as a device to make his hero's plight more pitiful, Sinclair had him find a job slaughtering animals at one of Chicago's large meat-packing plants. The brutal working conditions pictured were real—Sinclair had spent several months living near the stockyards and had found out more about the filth and horror behind the high fences than any other outsider ever had.

So his novel did shock millions of readers, though not quite as Sinclair had intended. Instead of being moved by his political message, they were outraged at the nauseating conditions in the plants where their steaks and roasts were processed.

Could *The Jungle* really be accurate? Even President Theodore Roosevelt wanted to know, and he sent a team of Department of Agriculture officials to investigate. When they reported that Sinclair had not exaggerated, the President put aside the political considerations that had kept him from throwing his full weight into the fight for a pure food and drug law. He let it be known that he wanted the law passed— and quickly.

Yet, even without special prodding from the White House, Congress was ready to act. Pressed by *Jungle* readers from every state, members of both houses quickly adopted a measure authorizing the Department of Agriculture to start inspecting the sanitary conditions in the meat-packing industry. They also passed the Pure Food and Drugs Act that had been pending for so many years. On June 30, 1906, President Roosevelt signed it into law.

But Dr. Wiley was not as happy as he had thought he would be. In the rush to get the bill through Congress, many compromises had been accepted. Still, it was a beginning! He set right to work planning how to enforce the new law.

3

Brane-Fude

The full name on the label was CUFORHEDAKE BRANE-FUDE.

Cure for a headache? Brain food? Did this pale liquid really contain sure relief for any headache sufferer and at the same time provide some special nourishment for the sufferer's brain? Was this preparation—in the words of the printed circular packed with every bottle—"a most wonderful, certain and harmless" product with "no poisonous ingredients of any kind"?

Dr. Wiley had his doubts about all these points. Furthermore, about two million bottles of Brane-Fude had been sold during the past twenty years, and the manufacturer not only had become rich on the proceeds but also had won a respected place among the business leaders of Washington, D.C.—he had even been elected president of the local chamber of commerce. If this man could become successful by fooling the public, others with similar ambitions were bound to feel encouraged. So there were many reasons why Dr. Wiley decided that he would use Brane-Fude as the first test of the power of the new Pure Food and Drugs Act.

Nobody was more aware than Dr. Wiley that the new law had grave weaknesses. To satisfy critics who preferred having no law at all, various provisions had been cut away by either the Senate or the House of Representatives. What was left merely set general guidelines.

The federal government was supposed to guard the purity of the nation's food supply, but no specific list of forbidden impurities was given. There was only a statement that no food should have any substance mixed or packed with it that would lower or injuriously affect its quality and strength. The problem of setting up rules about the use of particular preservatives or other substances was passed along to a committee composed of representatives from several government departments. Dr. Wiley feared that, in effect, this meant endless meetings with little prospect of any decisions.

On the matter of stopping the sale of worthless or dangerous medicines, the law's language was not quite as vague. It forbid the drug industry from making any claims for any remedy that were "false or misleading in any particular." If Brane-Fude did not fall into this category, Dr. Wiley thought, then nothing did.

So he set out to make an example of Brane-Fude and its manufacturer. Under the terms of the new law, violations were punishable by fine or imprisonment or both, after certain steps had been taken. No dealer could be prosecuted if he could produce a statement from his supplier certifying that the product in question justified the claims being made for it. This was intended to meet the objections of many business groups who were afraid that blameless merchants might otherwise be treated as criminals. But after the seizure of a suspected product, and after the completion of chemical tests justifying the original suspicion, and then after a hearing before the Secretary of Agriculture, if a manufacturer should still refuse to comply with the law voluntarily, then he could be hauled into federal court and put on trial.

It took nearly twenty months to go through all these

preliminary steps in the case against Brane-Fude. Finally, in February of 1908, a man named Robert N. Harper became the first citizen to be charged with violating the nation's Pure Food and Drugs Act.

Unlike a good many other manufacturers of patent medicines—so-called because they were patented, or sold under a registered trademark—Harper had never been a horse trainer or a carnival trickster. He had studied pharmacy at a Philadelphia college before setting up his business in the nation's capital. He knew enough about drugs to be aware that a substance called acetanilid had been discovered in Germany and had been found effective both in reducing fever and in deadening pain. So he made up a mixture of acetanilid and some other more ordinary pain-killers, dissolved his formula in an alcohol solution, then put it on the market late in the 1880's.

When Brane-Fude proved popular, Harper branched out and became a banker. He made some powerful political friends. For this reason, and also because he sincerely believed in the value of his headache remedy, he thought he had nothing to worry about when Dr. Wiley brought him into court.

Dr. Wiley's case was based on several different counts. The most serious was that acetanilid had not yet been proved harmless, nor had anyone definitely established how much of it could be safely swallowed. However, researchers had found evidence that seemed to indicate that in a frightening number of instances the substance could cause poisoning or even death.

Evidence to this effect was calmly brushed aside by Harper's lawyer. He put a professor of pharmacy from Columbia University on the witness stand and asked, "Professor, what is a lethal or fatal dose of acetanilid?"

"There is no such thing," this professor replied. Because he had studied in Germany with the chemist who had discovered the substance, he was honestly convinced of its value. He said that alleged cases of acetanilid poisoning probably had been caused by impurities also present in other medications, but that in his experience he found the Harper preparation to be perfectly safe. So Dr. Wiley had to accept the fact that medical experts differed on this point, and he was forced to stress some lesser points in his case.

The name "Cuforhedake," he said, implied that the medicine in question *cured* a headache, instead of just lessening the symptoms. Under the terms of the law this was a misleading claim, he contended, and the words "Brane-Fude" were even more misleading. Not only did the medicine not provide any nourishment for the brain, he said, but it could actually harm the brain.

"In what way?" Harper's attorney demanded.

"The alcohol in it tends to harden all the cells with which it comes in contact," Dr. Wiley replied.

It was on this narrow point that the judge hearing the case gave the jury clear advice. Unless they believed there was a particular kind of food that provided a particular nourishment for the human brain, a product labeled "Brane-Fude" had to be considered misleading under the Pure Food and Drugs Act. "This law was passed," the judge said, "not to protect experts especially, not to protect scientific men who know the meaning and value of drugs, but for the purpose of protecting ordinary citizens."

The jury arrived at a verdict promptly. They found Harper guilty, on the ground that he had misled the general public with the name he gave his product.

During the interval before the judge pronounced sentence on Harper, President Roosevelt took a personal hand in the case. He called the prosecuting attorney to the White House, and asked him to press not merely for a fine but for a jail term.

"This is a new law," President Roosevelt told newspaper reporters. "To a certain extent the court is blazing the way. It now remains to be seen whether this law is to be enforced, so that every manufacturer, every druggist—not merely in the District of Columbia, but in the whole land—will know that they must obey this law, that it was made for the benefit of the people of the United States."

Yet the judge refused to be guided by the opinion of the President. When the day for sentencing Harper arrived, the judge took note that the defendant promised to change the labels on his product in the future. For his past violation of the law, the judge levied fines totaling $700.

Dr. Wiley was outraged. "The man made two million dollars on the product," he fumed. "Now he's still $1,999,300 ahead."

Nevertheless, a trade journal for the drug industry printed an editorial noting that Harper's "money, position and influence were unable to save him from the stigma of conviction." The lesson the whole industry must learn, it said, "is that the law must be obeyed."

Dr. Wiley could not agree. He thought he had absorbed enough of the truth about politics during the past several years to prevent him from taking an unrealistic attitude on what could and what could not reasonably be expected to happen when powerful interests held opposing positions. Still, he was disgusted by the way Harper had managed to evade any real punishment. That President Roosevelt himself had tried to bring about a different outcome did not strike Dr. Wiley as particularly significant. If Roosevelt had a deep concern for the common good and was not just playing some political game involving the new law, he could have done a lot more, Dr. Wiley grumbled.

Why, consider the question of glucose, he would urge his friends. Glucose was the scientific name given to a sweetening produced by treating cornstarch with hydrochloric acid. Because this colorless syrup could be made cheaply, it was being used increasingly in jellies and other processed foods. The sale of plain bottled glucose for household use was also being pushed—but under another name. Corn syrup was what its manufacturers wanted to call it.

Dr. Wiley saw no reason to keep glucose off the market, for it appeared to be harmless. However, he saw no reason, either, for allowing it to be disguised as corn syrup. People ought to know exactly what they were getting, he insisted.

But "glucose" sounds like "glue," and people won't buy it, the food processors protested.

Too bad, said Dr. Wiley. Don't sell it if you don't like the sound of it.

Since the potential profit from this product was so great, the industry's leaders refused to accept Dr. Wiley's verdict. They carried their protest all the way to the White House, and President Roosevelt sided with them.

Summoning Dr. Wiley, the President warned him against trying to punish an industry unnecessarily. "You must make the manufacturers call a spade a spade," he said, "but don't make them call it a damn shovel."

Episodes like this had two effects. Even among his own staff, Dr. Wiley got a reputation for being too strict in his interpretation of the new law. At the same time, he began feeling less and less optimistic about his chances for accomplishing what he wanted.

Then when President Taft took over the White House, and gave even less attention to the pure food and drug measure,

Dr. Wiley became enraged. He began squabbling with some of his aides who urged him to calm down. But he could not. In a fit of anger about a committee decision ignoring his own ideas, he resigned from his government post.

He also broke his lifelong loyalty to the Republican Party, whose Presidents had so disappointed him, and began campaigning for the election of a Democratic professor of history —Woodrow Wilson—who was speaking out compellingly about the importance of reform, or change. Wilson wanted the public interest, rather than the special interests of the business community, to be the paramount factor in setting government policy. Dr. Wiley had all he could do to keep from waving his hat and hollering, "Hoorah!" when he heard Wilson talk.

During his last year in office, Dr. Wiley had shown more personal proof that he was still young in spirit. At the age of sixty-six, he married a librarian about half his own age. After he left the Department of Agriculture, Dr. Wiley and his wife settled on a farm near Washington. But he was in no mood to spend his time puttering around his property. While Mrs. Wiley delighted him by presenting him with one baby boy, and then another, he began a new career as a writer and lecturer.

In a monthly column for *Good Housekeeping* magazine and on the platform at women's club meetings, Dr. Wiley spoke freely about his favorite subject. Now that he was no longer restrained by governmental superiors warning him about upsetting business groups, he could say what he really thought—and he did.

If a product was labeled "boneless codfish," it should be absolutely boneless, he said. As long as any doubt at all remained about the safety of benzoate of soda, not a trace of this preservative ought to be allowed in ketchup, even if that meant housewives might have to go back to boiling their own tomato sauce. But he was confident, he added dryly, that once the ketchup makers were made to realize a suspected additive positively could not be used, they would be ingenious enough to find a safe substitute.

The pure-food enthusiasts who read his column and attended his lectures shared Dr. Wiley's single-minded outlook. They considered him a great man, and when he appeared on a platform, there was often thunderous applause as he was introduced as "the father of the Pure Food Law."

Nevertheless, the pioneering statute he had pushed through to passage back in 1906 far from fulfilled all the hopes of its supporters. Shortly before Dr. Wiley left office, Congress had plugged a loophole that had hampered enforcement of the drug section by adopting an amendment widening the definition of "misleading." Any false claim that a particular product could cure a particular ailment was declared to be a violation of the law, even if the manufacturer appeared sincere in his belief. Following the "Brane-Fude" case, a number of other manufacturers had been able to win "not guilty" verdicts on the grounds that they had not "knowingly" defrauded the public. Now this defense was no longer acceptable. Despite the new amendment, though, and despite President Wilson's dedication to "progress," Dr. Wiley and his friends had few occasions for cheering during the next decade.

One important new consumer protection was enacted in the early part of President Wilson's administration. With the steady growth of mass-production industries, and the accompanying growth of advertising, the carnival style of "pitchman" moved over into the advertising business. Willing to promise anything just to lure more customers in, the pitchman did not hesitate to shout outright lies.

"Gather around, folks," he would holler. "Now let me tell

you about the greatest boon to all mankind that has ever been invented. Do you see that powerful-looking fellow beside me? A few short months ago, he was so sick he couldn't even crawl, but then he found out about my secret herbs . . ."

When similar messages, printed in bold letters, began to bombard the public, the need for a method regulating advertising claims became apparent. In 1914, Congress had responded to other pressures by creating the Federal Trade Commission, which was empowered to control unfair competition under the antitrust acts, and the task of stopping deceptive ads was also assigned to the new agency. Exactly how this was to be accomplished was not made explicit, but the mere fact that the problem had been recognized and could now be grappled with was considered a sign of progress.

Besides this first effort of governmental regulation, a similar drive was started around the same time by business itself. In 1911, *Printer's Ink,* an advertising trade magazine, suggested that untruthful or deceptive advertising should be made a crime. A year later, the Associated Advertising Clubs of America set up a Vigilance Committee, which later became the National Better Business Bureau with local chapters in many parts of the country. The stated purpose of the BBB network was to discourage fraud in advertising and other dishonest business practices by establishing voluntary codes of ethical standards. But despite giving evidence that many businessmen did feel a sense of responsibility, this early attempt at self-policing had little impact.

Indeed, neither privately sponsored programs nor the efforts of public agencies had any substantial effect on the vast marketing picture confronting the American consumer during these years following Dr. Wiley's retirement. Only in the field of food could some activity be noted. The chemistry division of the Department of Agriculture, with a variety of soil-testing and other farm-related tasks besides its work on pure food and drugs, outgrew its basement laboratory and resettled in a new six-story building where a few thousand people worked on diverse investigations. Then, even this arrangement became unwieldly and the Food and Drug Administration was created to "administer" the Pure Food and Drugs Act.

Yet no matter how many technicians sat over Bunsen burners, no matter how diligently they conducted their experiments, the critical question was: Who set the agency's policy?

And it was not easy to answer that question. Despite devoted service by numerous experts, there was no Dr. Wiley to inflame the staff with crusading zeal, and his successors did their best to avoid controversy. Routine hearings were held, industry officials were summoned to appear and discuss possible abuses, but the agency's main thrust was on "educating" food processors, not on prosecuting the law's violators, or even deciding precisely what constituted a violation.

Still, public opinion did not seem to condemn the agency for inaction. The outbreak of World War I distracted people's attention from domestic problems, marking a turning point which became increasingly obvious as the years passed. Later the period from the opening of the twentieth century till 1914 became generally identified as the Progressive Era— a time when reform in many areas of national life captured the popular imagination. "Perhaps what was most remarkable about the Progressives was their ability to sustain reformist enthusiasm as long as they did," a leading historian wrote. As a result, only aging Progressives like Dr. Wiley still felt strongly about pure food during the 1920's.

As far as the majority of people were concerned, the mere fact that there was a pure food and drugs act on the books meant there was no cause for alarm. Secure in their belief that now the government was doing all that had to be done, they could buy whatever they chose without worrying about its purity. Besides this comfortable—if not very careful—attitude, there was another basis for the prevailing apathy.

"The business of America is business," was the opinion of President Calvin Coolidge, and most of his fellow citizens agreed with him. When the end of World War I failed to bring about a new era of international good feeling, many Americans were so disillusioned that they turned their backs on anyone who talked about world problems or even domestic ones. They put all their energy into making money, and they were sure they were right because so many people were making more money than ever before.

With ordinary workmen buying cars and new millionaires buying yachts, why should the system be questioned? It seemed positively unpatriotic to suggest that American industry was less than perfect. While the stock market was booming, only a handful of radicals dared to offer any such criticism.

However, two critics did manage to stir a few ripples in 1927. They were Stuart Chase, an economist as well as a lively writer, and an engineer named F. J. Schlink, who had spent several years working for the National Bureau of Standards, a federal agency that had been set up to save taxpayers' money by testing hundreds of products before their purchase by other governmental units. Not until the 1970's did the idea of publishing the results of these tests so that taxpayers could save money on their own purchases strike many consumers as sensible. Even then, only a start was made in issuing lists of approved items because of various objections from business executives and government officials. But nearly half a century earlier, Chase and Schlink had raised the point in a book they called *Your Money's Worth*.

In its pages, they also charged that "slick salesmanship" was pushing many people to pay excessive prices for items that were not even needed. "We are all Alices," they wrote, "in a Wonderland of conflicting claims, bright promises, fancy packages, soaring words and almost impenetrable ignorance."

Even those shoppers who did try to do their buying intelligently were hardly better off than the most indifferent consumer, Chase and Schlink said, since a large number of the products on the market were too new or too complicated for the layman to appraise without the aid of highly sophisticated testing devices. The housewife who bought a loaf of bread in a store could compare it with a home-baked loaf, but she had no standard by which to measure the various brands of electric toasters.

"You're right!" thousands of readers wrote to the authors. "But what can we *do* about it?"

The result was that Schlink started a new organization in 1929. Patterned after the government-operated Bureau of Standards, it was intended to conduct impartial tests of various consumer products, then to publicize the results in a magazine that would be issued monthly. Schlink called his new group Consumers' Research; the magazine was *Consumer Bulletin.*

Due to problems involved in raising money, setting up test laboratories, and attracting subscribers, *Consumer Bulletin* did not reach a great number of people. Within a few years, problems concerning policy-making caused part of Schlink's staff to break away and form another testing service they called Consumers Union; its monthly magazine was *Consumer Reports.* But neither the original group nor its offshoot was able to attract more than about fifty thousand subscribers apiece. Their appeal seemed to extend no further than those serious-minded teachers and other well-educated shoppers who were ready to think of themselves as "consumers." In the popular mind, the word had a vaguely unpleasant tinge, conjuring up a picture of a penny-pinching busybody with no faith in American industry.

But it was not the appearance of the first consumer magazine that made 1929 a significant date in the history of consumerism; that was the year of the great stock-market crash which sent waves of panic across the United States and then most other industrialized countries. Month after month, more and more people lost their jobs. As factories everywhere shut down, long lines of desperate men formed in many cities. With their families starving, they stood waiting for emergency rations of free soup. Some men too proud to seek charity tried to earn a few dollars by selling apples on street corners. Suddenly a large number of Americans lost their faith in American industry. And even those who were fortunate enough to be still working had to watch how they spent every penny.

In this new atmosphere of fear, once again it was a book that aroused public opinion to the point of demanding better protection for the nation's consumers.

4

The Chamber of Horrors

In 1933 the population of the United States had just about reached the one hundred million mark, so nobody could mistake the meaning of the title, *100,000,000 Guinea Pigs*. But what sort of experiments were being tried out on every American man, woman, and child?

To ensure that merely a glance at the book's cover would answer this question, its publishers added a few words of explanation—"Dangers in Everyday Foods, Drugs and Cosmetics." They hoped this would stir the curiosity of the casual reader and cause him or her to buy a copy. Yet even the publisher had no idea just how many people would be stirred. Despite the financial hardships so widely experienced during the depths of the Depression, this book sold so phenomenally that it went through thirty-six printings.

Thousands of people were horrified when they read the case histories collected by the authors, the same F. J. Schlink who had founded Consumers' Research, and Arthur Kallet, an engineer for Schlink's group, who later headed the rival Consumers Union. From their own investigations and from reports of various medical and governmental units, they put together a real rogues' gallery, depicting dozens of unsavory characters, such as a former car thief who switched to peddling poisonous radium salts as a reputable cure-all.

"Any scoundrel who takes it into his head to enter the food or drug business can experiment on us," Schlink and Kallet wrote. "He may be uneducated, even feeble-minded. If he decides to become a manufacturer, it is his privilege to take down a dozen bottles from a shelf, mix their contents together, advertise the mixture as a remedy for indigestion, or asthma, or coughs, and persuade us to buy it. The mix may contain strychnine, arsenic, carbolic acid, and other deadly poisons. But—in most states—he will have violated no law."

For the Pure Food and Drugs Act of 1906 had "such huge loopholes," the authors said, that all Americans had been "forced into the role of laboratory guinea pigs."

Even where food was concerned, the public had much less protection than it imagined, Schlink and Kallet contended. According to their angry bill of particulars, eating hamburger in many diners was about as safe as getting meat out of a garbage can standing in the hot sun. Americans who ate dried fruits were swallowing poisonous preservatives that had long since been outlawed in France and Japan. Many fresh fruits and vegetables were tainted by dangerous sprays used to protect crops from insect damage.

For even in the case of foods, a manufacturer was not required to prove that the substances he added were safe, the authors pointed out. "His customers, by dying or becoming ill in large numbers—and in such a way that the illness can be traced directly to the foodstuff involved and to no other cause—must first prove it is harmful before any action will be considered."

Yet it was not surprising that the Food and Drug Administration was so ineffective, Schlink and Kallet said. It was supposed to police 110,000 different items sold all over the country, but it had a grand total of only sixty-five inspectors.

What could be done to improve matters? "Above all," the book advised, "let your voice be heard loudly and often." This advice met a ready response, particularly from women's groups and from some of the labor unions whose role in American life was expanding rapidly under the New Deal program of President Franklin Roosevelt, recently elected in 1932. The women and the workers provided the nucleus for a new sort of special interest group on the American scene— the consumer movement.

Until the New Deal era, some individuals and even some groups had taken a particular interest in consumer problems. A small but vocal National Consumers League had been founded back in 1899, but its main effort during its early days was devoted to the side issue of endorsing fair working conditions for the men and women who produced such consumer products as clothing, rather than to consumer interests as such. It took the Depression to bring about a unified consumer front large enough to be described as a mass movement.

President Roosevelt himself recognized what was happening. "I believe," he said, "that we are at the threshold of a fundamental change in our popular economic thought, that in the future we are going to think less about the producer and more about the consumer."

An assistant secretary of agriculture, Rexford G. Tugwell, adopted as his own special challenge the improvement of the lot of the American consumer. Like Dr. Wiley, whose Poison Squad had injected high drama into a complicated legislative battle, Tugwell made good use of a similar dramatic weapon. His was the "Chamber of Horrors."

It was actually an exhibit of posters, bottles, and labels illustrating many of the points that been made in *100,000,000*

Guinea Pigs. Probably the most gripping was a poster show-ing before-and-after pictures of a pretty teenager from Ohio whose eyes had been turned totally blind by the aniline dye in an eyelash "beautifier."

Because the original Pure Food and Drugs Act omitted any mention of cosmetics, Tugwell's campaign for a new law emphasized the importance of including all kinds of beauty aids. He also stressed the need for expanding the meaning of the word "drugs" to include allegedly curative devices of every description. Many of these so-called miracle cures were weird combinations of coils and motors that looked impres-sive to people who knew very little about science. "They are the kind of device a ten-year-old boy would build to fool an eight-year-old," one physics expert told Tugwell.

However, Tugwell wanted such drastic changes in nearly every section of the original law that even Dr. Wiley would have shaken his head if he had still been alive. He had died in 1930, just short of his eighty-sixth birthday.

What Tugwell wanted was nothing less than a complete revamping of the 1906 measure, giving government inspec-tors much broader powers and setting much stiffer penalties for even well-meaning violators. These proposals would have made the Food and Drug Administration so powerful that any man with Dr. Wiley's experience could easily have pre-dicted the reaction that followed. The howls of outrage that rose from industry spokesmen made the protests against the original law seem mild by comparison. But the strictness of the new regulation was not the only reason for all this clamor. There was also the general political climate of the country.

Ever since the Russian Revolution of 1917 had set up a Communist dictatorship there, the threat that Communism might spread all the way to the United States had alarmed many Americans. A number of President Roosevelt's New

Deal policies struck conservative citizens as dangerous opening wedges for the hated Soviet system, and no other measure provoked more of this "anti-Red" feeling than the one Tugwell sponsored.

This was partly a result of his personal beliefs. As a professor of economics at Columbia University before he had joined Roosevelt's "Brain Trust"—the sarcastic name some newspapers gave the group of college professors responsible for planning many New Deal policies—Tugwell had made no secret of his radical theories. He said openly that "property rights and financial rights" ought to be considered less important than "human rights." He was a Socialist, he said, but to many American businessmen that was the same as being an outright Communist.

So the battle in the 1930's for the passage of a new pure food law was even more bitter than the battle three decades earlier. On one side was virtually every business group of any importance, all calling the proposed measure "un-American." Among the milder witnesses who spoke against the bill at congressional hearings was a food processor who said, "If a criminal is believed to be in a house with nine other men who may be innocent of any wrongdoing, do we surround the house with police and shoot down every man in it to make sure the criminal will not escape?" A spokesman for the wholesale drug industry was much angrier. "I have never in my life read a bill or heard of a bill so grotesque in its terms, evil in its purpose, and vicious in its possible consequences," he said.

One particular section in the bill generated the most heated protests. Included at the special request of Schlink and his friends, it called for the setting of federal standards to help buyers make their choices intelligently. If under the terms of the new measure a can of peaches were to be labeled

"Grade A," every shopper could be assured that the peaches in the can would meet specific requirements as to appearance and quality. In like manner, fruit that met less exacting standards would be labeled "Grade B" or even "Grade C," regardless of the brand name under which it was sold. Although in Schlink's mind this kind of grade labeling would do no more than protect a consumer from paying a high price for an inferior product, most food processors thought otherwise. To them, compulsory grade labeling would mean the end of brand names. They called this plan a plot to limit the American housewife's freedom to make her own decisions, and claimed that it would surely lead to a "dull uniformity" on the nation's store shelves.

Grade labeling was singled out as a clear indication of the real purpose of the young consumer movement. "It is a movement," one industry leader said, "that has been organized by men posing as protectors of the consumer, but its basic aim is to attack American businessmen, their methods and their products." The end result, he insisted, could only be to undermine the whole American system of free enterprise.

On the other side, trying to defend Tugwell's bill, were representatives of various groups making their first concerted effort on behalf of American consumers. Having little experience as lobbyists seeking to influence the members of Congress, they found themselves at quite a disadvantage. They were hampered by their lack of knowledge about the fine points of politics, and also had a difficult time getting publicity. Because newspaper and magazine publishers were so dependent on the revenue received from advertising, these molders of public opinion were very careful not to offend major advertisers.

Under the circumstances, the Chamber of Horrors became

a valuable tool for the pro-Tugwell forces. Housed in a large cabinet with glass doors, it was transported from meeting to meeting whenever there was any possibility of influencing voters to put pressure on their congressmen. At Chicago's "Century of Progress" Fair in the summer of 1934, it was one of the displays that attracted the most attention. Mrs. Eleanor Roosevelt, departing from the pattern set by former First Ladies, was deeply involved in seeking solutions for many social problems. She devoted some of her daily newspaper columns to the food and drug exhibit.

Nevertheless, several sessions of Congress produced action that could only be described as negative. In the course of the hearings, one provision after another was chopped out of Tugwell's proposed law. New York Senator Royal S. Copeland, who was acting as floor leader of efforts to secure the bill's approval, rose in disgust one day to tell the Senate:

> Every slimy serpent of a vile manufacturer of patent medicine is right now working his wiggling way around this Capitol. I have heard heretofore about the effort dear old Dr. Wiley made to secure the passage of the original law twenty-eight years ago. Historically I was familiar with it, but now from experience I am familiar with it. I know the devious ways of those who are seeking to defeat the effort of the Congress to give protection to the health and lives of our people.

But, despite his tone of bitterness, Senator Copeland had a far better grasp of political reality than Dr. Wiley had ever had. He cannily made many compromises during the extended committee hearings. He understood perfectly well that Tugwell's original draft had been much too strong to win the support of a majority of his fellow lawmakers, and he had some doubts himself about the wisdom of giving any federal agency the extensive powers Tugwell had wanted to give the Food and Drug Administration. Thus, for several years in a row, Senator Copeland conducted a series of strategic retreats, surrendering sections of the proposed measure that he did not think were essential.

However, the bill's opponents still showed no signs of being satisfied. It began to appear that, after all, there would not be any changes made in the 1906 law. Then another of those unpredictable events that have such a startling effect on the course of history occurred. Every newspaper in the country printed terrifying headlines about the "Elixir Sulfanilamide Scandal."

Sulfanilamide was a "miracle drug" that had only recently come into general use in the treatment of pneumonia and other diseases. Practically everybody had heard of some case where a doctor had prescribed it for a patient on the brink of death and the patient had miraculously recovered. Then, during a few weeks in 1937, alarming stories began to spread about patients with comparatively minor ailments who died soon after taking sulfanilamide.

Emergency inquiries disclosed that all the patients who had died had been given a particular brand of the drug, distributed by a small company in Tennessee. This company's product was sold under the trade name of "Elixir Sulfanilamide," elixir being a word commonly used by druggists to signify a medicine in an alcohol solution. Although an elixir can be quite harmless, there are complex chemical differences in the various liquids that have the same general properties. Was it possible that in this case the particular elixir, rather than the drug dissolved in it, was at fault?

It was. Federal officials soon were able to report that a chemist working for the Tennessee company had got the idea of using a new substance—diethylene glycol—as the solvent for sulfanilamide in his firm's product. Without troubling to study scientific journals for any evidence of this solvent's effect on the human system, he had tested it only for fragrance and flavor—not for safety. There was nothing in the Pure Food and Drugs Act of 1906 that required him to do otherwise, or to list diethylene glycol as an ingredient on the product's label.

Thus, even physicians who happened to be familiar with studies questioning the safety of this substance were unaware of its presence when they prescribed Elixir Sulfanilamide for their patients. Fortunately, only two thousand pints of the mixture had been made before the Food and Drug Administration rushed into action. Its agents swiftly traced and seized all but ninety-three pint bottles, which had already been sold by druggists.

Yet these ninety-three bottles had taken a frightful toll. Their contents had killed a total of 107 people.

When the whole story of this medical tragedy was pieced together and printed, shock waves spread in every direction. The chemist responsible for mixing the murderous medicine committed suicide. A mother whose six-year-old daughter had died in horrible pain after being given the elixir wrote to President Roosevelt, begging him to see that other children were saved from similar suffering. For reasons of political convenience, the President had been letting his assistant secretary of agriculture assume most of the burden of sponsoring a new pure food and drug law, but now Roosevelt took personal command of the campaign.

The result was that both the Senate and the House of Representatives finally stopped their delaying tactics. On June 25, 1938, a new Food, Drug and Cosmetic Act went into effect.

There was little rejoicing, though, among those who had been fighting hardest for reform. Assistant Secretary Tugwell, dismayed by the long struggle, had recently resigned his government post. Senator Copeland, his health deteriorated from the strenuous efforts he had put into the battle, collapsed on the last night of the debate and died without knowing whether the bill would pass. Schlink and Kallet and some other leaders of the consumer cause were so unhappy about the compromises adopted during the final push to win approval that they actually urged President Roosevelt to veto the bill.

Nevertheless, the 1938 law did contain several important new safeguards. Cosmetics and mechanical contrivances that were sold as health restorers came under federal regulation for the first time. A number of provisions in the original law of 1906 were strengthened along the lines Tugwell had suggested—the requirements for avoiding prosecution on the grounds of providing false or misleading labels, for instance, were made much stricter. Some new powers were given to the Food and Drug Administration, notably the power to move swiftly, by means of a court order called an injunction, which permitted immediate seizure of the suspected product even as time-consuming chemical tests were being carried out.

However, there was no provision for grade labeling. And although preliminary tests were required before a new drug could be put on the market, this section of the law was much weaker than the consumer spokesmen had wanted it to be. So were the sections setting penalties for violators.

Still, there were many people who thought the new law was the best that could be expected in a society in which the interests of business groups as well as consumer groups had to be taken into consideration. This attitude was widely held in the Food and Drug Administration, but the agency was by no means as unwilling to make enemies as its severest critics claimed. Less than a month after the new bill was passed, the Administration used its new powers dramatically.

No exhibit in the Chamber of Horrors had caused more shudders than the pictures of the Ohio girl who had been blinded by an eyelash "beautifier." Making the first seizure authorized under the terms of the new law, agents from the FDA swooped down on the manufacturer and carted away the entire stock of this gruesome product.

But horrors on a far greater scale were soon absorbing America's attention. Across the Atlantic Ocean, Hitler and his Nazi storm troops had been moving beyond the borders of Germany. The Nazi seizure of Austria and Czechoslovakia was followed by an attack on Poland, and at last England and France saw no course except to fight in defense of freedom. The outbreak of the Second World War in 1939 had a grave impact on the United States.

Despite the disillusion left by World War I, and despite the fact that many Americans still wanted no part of Europe's problems, suddenly even those who were in favor of remaining isolated from the new conflict saw the need for building up America's defenses. Purely domestic concerns, such as food and drug protection, were crowded out of the newspapers. When the situation in Europe grew more critical, with the fall of France and the beginning of fierce bombing raids on England's cities, American interest in the conflict abroad increased still further. Japan's air strike against Pearl Harbor, bringing the United States into the war in 1941, completed the eclipse of ordinary, peacetime business as usual. Every ounce of the national energy went to strengthening the nation's war effort.

That did not mean, though, that the word "consumer" disappeared from use. On the contrary, it had never before been used so often and in so many different connections, for the Depression had given it a permanent place in the national vocabulary. In setting up war emergency boards of various kinds—new local, state, and federal agencies with some specific task related to the war—public officials at every level of government almost always appointed at least one member who was supposed to represent consumers, while the rest of the panel represented assorted other segments of public opinion.

Yet, for a number of reasons, these consumer representatives made hardly any impression. In the first place, they were usually women, and it was generally assumed by their male associates that they were neither as well informed nor as reasonable as men were. Added to this widespread prejudice was the fact that consumer representatives did not really represent any specific group in the same sense that a dairy farmer could speak for all the producers of milk products, or that a railroad president could speak for his whole industry. Many of the consumer representatives were teachers of home economics or public-spirited housewives who did not even belong to an organization, so they could easily be brushed aside on the grounds that they spoke only for themselves.

No wonder, then, that the comparatively few deep believers in the cause of consumerism felt discouraged during the war. Despite all the talk they heard about the importance of considering the consumer viewpoint, they saw small evidence that consumer interests were being taken seriously. The picture, however, was not entirely bleak.

The biggest of all the emergency war agencies on the home front was the Office of Price Administration—the OPA, as almost everybody called it. With its headquarters in Washington, but with branches in every part of the country, the OPA had more control over the making of routine household decisions than any other governmental unit had ever had before the war, or has had since its end. Not only did it have the power to set the prices shoppers paid for almost all goods and services, but it also could decide how much of any product that was in short supply a particular family could buy—how much sugar, how many cans of soup, how many pairs of shoes. Gasoline and tires for all civilian autos were also rationed by the OPA. In effect, the OPA was the most powerful consumer organization the nation had ever known.

For without the OPA or some similar agency to enforce price ceilings, the pressure of wartime shortages would surely have pushed prices higher and higher. Those consumers least able to pay high prices would have been kept from buying, while rich consumers would be able to get more than their fair share of scarce items. The mere fact that the OPA was established, and that it functioned as well as it did, represented a triumph for the consumer movement.

At the same time, Mrs. Eleanor Roosevelt and some other outspoken advocates of the consumer cause helped to give consumerism a broader base. Ever since the 1930's, courses exploring "consumer problems" had been taught in more and more high schools, but they had tended to concentrate on the narrow and not overly fascinating topic of how to save pennies by shopping intelligently. Now there were discussions about more interesting aspects of the subject. How could deprived minority groups be protected from price-gouging merchants? What could be done to deter manufacturers who tried to palm off inferior merchandise at inflated prices? Were food processors paying proper attention to preserving the nutritional value of bread and other basic foods?

In New York and a few other large cities, the consumer movement showed its first signs of militancy during the war. There were scattered episodes where housewives or union members picketed some store protesting against the poor quality of its potatoes or the unfairness of its installment-buying contracts. By and large, though, most Americans were far too engrossed in winning the war to worry much about other matters.

But if consumer-minded women, and the comparatively small number of men who shared their interest, thought that the coming of peace would bring a rebirth of popularity to consumerism, they could hardly have been more mistaken. Nothing of the sort happened—at least not right away.

5

Undercurrents

About 10 per cent of the students attending high school toward the end of World War II studied some kind of "consumer education" before they graduated. Of this number, the great majority were girls, for the subject was usually presented under the general heading of home economics. If the units treating consumerism had been a separate course rather than just part of a survey course covering the many aspects of household management, the title could well have been simply, "How to Buy."

Budgets. Comparison shopping. Did pillow cases made of percale last as long as pillow cases made of muslin? The topics covered by these units were hardly fascinating to most girls, and the teachers who taught them were often on the stodgy side. But there was a more important reason why these well-intentioned efforts had little effect.

Once World War II ended, almost everyone who had any money went on a great spending spree. Buy! Buy! Buy! There seemed to be no other aim anywhere in the land. No one seemed to care about following rules for intelligent buying. Cash registers kept ringing up new sales, and consumer specialists told each other that the nation was engaged in an orgy of buying.

They should not have been surprised, however. During the war, many products like cars and refrigerators had been unavailable because factories had been converted to produce tanks or airplane parts. Many other items had all but disappeared from the stores because the armed forces had priority over any civilian needs. Even clothing had been manufactured in limited styles and quantities for the home front, while the industry struggled to fill military orders.

When the first postwar cars began rolling off the assembly lines, people in every town and city all but besieged dealer showrooms. The prospective buyers had to put their names on long lists, and hoped to receive delivery within the year if they were lucky. It wasn't uncommon to hear stories about people who tried to bribe dealers by handing them wads of dollar bills "under the table" in exchange for having their names put near the top of the list.

So most people naturally gave little thought to comparing the workmanship on different models of cars, or to the safety features, or to anything else that might make one auto a better value than another. All they wanted was a new car as quickly as possible—preferably the sharpest and the newest-looking car in the lot. They had had enough of their drab old buggy throughout the war years.

Even when the first rush finally tapered off, people still seemed bent on buying. Now that it was possible to trade in an "old" model every year or two, and get the latest one dreamed up by Detroit, the auto business kept booming. And much to the disgust of consumers who put a premium on quality rather than outward appearance, the average person still seemed more influenced by showy styling than solid workmanship. This was the era of splashy two-tone paint jobs, of enormous fender fins jutting out over rear bumpers.

"Dangerous to pedestrians!" cried the rare auto-buyer who cared about such matters. "Impractical to repair!"

But thoughtful consumers had many other worries besides cars. New houses featuring a façade of fake brick sold so fast that few builders bothered to nail the roof down securely. After being forced during the war years to wear simple dresses designed to save fabric, women blossomed forth in a "new look" every season. Even clothes washers stressed styling features more than the plain facts about their washday performance.

Nevertheless, there were some undercurrents during the carefree fifties that gave serious consumers reasons to hope the prevailing climate would not last. Professors of economics and other opinion molders began to discuss several basic questions.

Who *is* a consumer?

What were the legitimate boundaries for consumer interests in the modern world?

How should consumers go about playing their proper role in a highly industrialized country like the United States?

On the fundamental matter of defining who was a consumer, a curious point often overlooked now received attention. More and more teachers were asking their students, "Are *you* a consumer?" Often the only response was a baffled stare, and then the teacher might say, "That's right! Nobody really thinks of himself—or herself—as a consumer. Nobody says, 'I'm a consumer,' the way they would say, 'I'm a farmer,' or a truck driver, or even a housewife. Still, the fact remains that we're all consumers. And there you have the nub of the problem. Everybody is a consumer, even though nobody is a consumer."

This point was sometimes put in more sophisticated economic language, but the gist of it was repeated often and it won increasing acceptance. No matter that most people played many different roles in their daily life, they were still consumers.

Then what were the special interests of consumers? In the past it had been generally accepted that since the consumer was merely a user of various products, consumer interests had to do solely with buying those products at a fair price. Now that no longer appeared to cover the subject. If everybody was a consumer, all questions, even those indirectly related to buying practices, became a reasonable subject for a consumer's concern. Why were certain products—such as two-tone cars with tail fins—readily available, while others that made more sense from the viewpoint of the public interest were not? What else besides outright need made people make up their minds to buy a particular product? Was it good or bad for the country as a whole if the business community had the sole right to decide such matters of public policy as whether detergents should be substituted for soap? Many people summed up the answers in a short but broad statement: any business practice involving the public interest belonged under the heading of a consumer problem.

But could the great unorganized mass of consumers play an effective part in an economy dominated by big business?

According to Adam Smith, an Englishman who had gained a lasting influence on both sides of the Atlantic by writing a book called *The Wealth of Nations* back in 1776, the consumer really was the most important factor in a free economy. "Consumption is the sole end and purpose of all production," he wrote, "and the interest of the producer ought to be attended to, only so far as it may be necessary for promoting that of the consumer." He based this opinion on the belief that consumers in the long run had full control over what was and was not produced because they alone could decide whether or not they wanted to buy a product. He felt sure the strength of consumer demand for a particular product was one of the two decisive factors in setting a fair price, the other being the available supply of the product.

People with a deep faith in the wisdom of the past still took comfort from Adam Smith's view of the consumer as uncrowned king of the marketplace. But during the 1950's some economists began to express doubts whether consumers retained their traditional power over modern giant corporations, whose strength was increased by skillful advertising. These doubters thought new techniques were needed to restore the traditional balance between consumers and producers.

As early as 1954, Governor Averell S. Harriman of New York appointed the nation's first official spokesman for consumers—actually a spokeswoman, Dr. Persia Campbell, a professor of economics at Queens College. Five years elapsed, though, before California created the country's second post of this description.

Meanwhile, Dr. Campbell provided a pioneering demonstration of what a consumer advisor to a state governor could do. As a member of the governor's cabinet, she sat in on hearings to consider rate increases requested by commuter railroads. She worked to secure passage of a new law bringing time-payment purchases of all consumer goods under state control for the first time. She held conferences with the leaders of many industries—"What I try to get across to the merchants of the state is that honesty does pay, and if they deal fairly with the consumer, business will be bigger and better than ever." She also supervised educational programs aimed at consumers themselves, including the preparation of leaflets on subjects ranging from "Know Value in Clothing" to "Read the Label on Dangerous Substances and Avoid Tragedy."

But although Dr. Campbell did achieve passage of a law putting installment buying under at least limited control, for the most part her accomplishments could be measured only in terms of getting publicity. Beyond stirring some new interest in consumer problems, she made hardly any impression within her own state, let alone around the rest of the country. For the time was not yet ripe for a reversal of the postwar attitude of complacency, as Senator Guy Gillette of Iowa also discovered.

Seeking the Senate's approval for a plan to set up a new committee on consumer interests, he was opposed on three grounds: first, there already were government agencies that "adequately" represented the consumer; second, the Senate already had too many committees; and third, a person's interests as a consumer could not really be separated from his interests as a farmer or a worker or an employer.

Despite the seeming contradictions between the first and third points, and despite the lack of any noticeable pressure from the general public favoring new consumer protections, Senator Gillette and a few sympathetic colleagues did not feel too discouraged. In the pages of publications addressed specifically to business groups, they found ample evidence that the pendulum must soon begin to swing in the opposite direction.

"Search out the consumer and attack him!" This was the message being spread more and more widely among sales executives and throughout the advertising industry. Advances in the social sciences—especially psychology, which examined the reasons why people behaved as they did, and sociology, which studied many aspects of group behavior—had brought some startling changes to the marketplace. Instead of just urging people to buy a particular product, advertisements prepared for the new medium of television, and also for radio, newspapers, and magazines, were using the results of scientific research about people's inner motives. But Gillette thought that as soon as the public realized that it was being attacked by these new weapons, it was bound to react sharply.

Then in 1957 a book called *The Hidden Persuaders* gave thousands of Americans their first inkling of this trend. Written at white heat by Vance Packard, an expert journalist, it exposed the methods being used by many mass-production industries to play upon the secret fears and desires buried within the human mind.

Citing specific examples ranging from cars to soft drinks, Packard showed how the basic human drives uncovered by psychologists were being appealed to by the makers and sellers of many well-known brands. For instance, some auto models that stressed power and had been given aggressive-sounding names were supposed to attract masculine buyers who felt frustrated by the dull routine of their daily lives. And most soft drinks attempted in their advertising to imply that since popular people drank a particular beverage, others drinking it would surely be popular too. More unpleasantly, the makers of some products like mouthwashes were doing their best to create new fears in order to raise the figures on their sales charts. Such themes were not adopted at random. A whole new area of inquiry, known as "motivational research," had been expanding rapidly to satisfy industry's desire to learn more about the ways of luring consumers.

One of the basic ingredients in the American character, though, was still rugged individualism. *The Hidden Persuaders* caused a widespread reaction. Many readers did not at all like the idea that their inner thoughts were being manipulated to make them buy a product. They much preferred to feel that they were coming to such conclusions on their own. And so the undercurrents feeding a revival of consumerism came closer to the surface.

Among the first clear signs of this was a spectacular coup by the Food and Drug Administration. In a sense a barometer registering the prevailing feeling about consumer problems, the FDA had been carrying on its regular activities quietly, doing nothing to call attention to itself. Then suddenly, shortly before Thanksgiving 1959, the agency exploded into the news. It seized a large part of the nation's recently harvested cranberry crop and destroyed it.

This drastic action had been taken, the FDA said, because the cranberries had been sprayed with chemicals that apparently were causing the rats in some laboratory tests to develop cancer.

Irate protests flared up. Similar chemical sprays had been used for years without any adverse effects on human beings, cranberry growers insisted. And the animal tests were far from conclusive. Under the circumstances, it was unfair and even unpatriotic to keep cranberry sauce off America's holiday dinner tables. Not only the industry most directly affected but also many other food suppliers and business spokesmen joined in a loud chorus of complaints about the FDA's unexpected crackdown.

Applause came, though, from several other directions. There was still no steady clamor for increased consumer protections, but many people were beginning to show interest—by speaking up at diverse meetings or by writing letters to newspapers and to lawmakers. Now that the political wind was so obviously shifting, the FDA was perfectly safe in taking a step it might not have dared to risk taking just a few years earlier. To steer a course favoring consumer goals was becoming much easier.

Nobody knew this better than a homespun senator from Tennessee named Estes Kefauver.

6

Three K's for the Consumer

Senator Kefauver wanted to be President of the United States. Clapping a coonskin cap on his head to emphasize his folksy country background, he had tried repeatedly to win the Democratic nomination. But a youthful senator from Massachusetts who also had Presidential ambitions would not step aside. His name was John F. Kennedy.

Kennedy and Kefauver—two men more different in their personal style would not be easy to find. But besides answering roll calls at the same point in the alphabet, they shared something else. Over and above their own private feelings of rivalry, they both supported the cause of consumerism.

While he was campaigning for election in the autumn of 1960, Kennedy spoke vigorously on the subject. "The consumer is the only man in our economy without a high-powered lobbyist," he said. "I intend to be that lobbyist."

After he was elected President, Kennedy took more than a year to keep his promise, but when he finally did—in March of 1962—he did it handsomely. He sent Congress a special message setting forth the broadest program of consumer protections that had ever been proposed. He called it the "Consumer Bill of Rights." These four rights, as described by President Kennedy, included:

1. The right to safety—to be protected against the marketing of goods which are hazardous to health or life.
2. The right to be informed—to be protected against fraudulent, deceitful, or grossly misleading information, advertising, labeling, or other practices, and to be given the facts needed to make an informed choice.
3. The right to choose—to be assured, wherever possible, access to a variety of products and services at competitive prices; and in those industries where competition is not workable and government regulation is substituted, an assurance of satisfactory quality and service at fair prices.
4. The right to be heard—to be assured that consumer interest will receive full and sympathetic consideration in the formulation of government policy, and fair and expeditious treatment in its administrative tribunals.

Toward these ends, Kennedy urged Congress to help him improve existing consumer programs by providing more funds for the agencies in charge of them. Besides the Food and Drug Administration and the Federal Trade Commission, he listed at least a dozen other governmental units with specific responsibilities in some area of vital concern to consumers, ranging from meat inspection—handled by the Department of Agriculture—to prosecuting mail frauds—a duty of the post office.

Then President Kennedy went on to the real core of his program. He asked Congress to pass a series of new laws expanding the role of the federal government in protecting the nation's consumers from sharp business practices. Among these measures, three were already stirring wide controversy.

Each had its own sponsor who was attempting to steer it through to final approval.

Senator Paul H. Douglas of Illinois was trying to win friends for a bill setting federal guidelines to regulate money-lending. His aim was to protect borrowers from having to pay exorbitant interest rates and from being victimized in other ways by banks and loan companies and by merchants who sold goods on the installment plan.

"Truth-in-Lending" was the phrase news analysts had coined to give a simple explanation of a highly complicated piece of legislation, but even the catchy title did not seem likely to save the bill from being buried under the weight of adverse testimony by business interests. In their eyes, Senator Douglas was trespassing on an area rightfully reserved for private enterprise. If any abuses did exist, they could best be corrected by the business groups that were most familiar with the problem, spokesmen for these groups insisted.

At the same time, Senator Philip A. Hart of Michigan was pressing for another set of federal guidelines. His measure, which aimed to stop manufacturers from putting their products in odd-sized boxes or otherwise confusing and misleading the unwary buyer, had been tagged the "Truth-in-Packaging" bill. But its chances for success seemed equally dim in the face of concentrated fire from the nation's retailers and also from practically every industry that sold its products on supermarket shelves where package design was such an important factor in capturing a shopper's attention.

The third major law to which President Kennedy committed his prestige as a "lobbyist" was being sponsored by Senator Kefauver. Despite their former rivalry, the President went out of his way to support the Tennessee lawmaker's special project.

As far back as 1957, Senator Kefauver had begun investigating what effect the rising number of business mergers was having on the ordinary consumer. Did a handful of large companies control the steel industry? the auto industry? the bread-baking industry? In each case, Kefauver satisfied himself that the classic definition of a monopoly applied, with a few giant companies accounting for such a big share of the total product that they could easily set almost any price level they cared to, without worrying about either resistance from consumers or competition from other manufacturers. But a comparatively small industry appeared to provide the worst example of the way monopolistic practices could hurt the ordinary citizen. Kefauver was soon concentrating on it.

It was the wholesale drug industry, which mainly confined itself to making the medicines sold by doctors' prescription. If it was relatively small in terms of total sales, it was quite the opposite in terms of profits. For instance, an Atlantic City druggist testified before Senator Kefauver's subcommittee on monopoly practices that in 1939 he had paid $1,000 for some shares of stock in one of the drug companies he dealt with, and the market value of this investment, by 1958, had reached the astronomical figure of $447,000.

The mere fact that the owners of drug companies could reap such enormous profits raised suspicions in Senator Kefauver's mind—suspicions that the industry was charging needlessly high prices for its products. Yet even he was astonished by the figures some witnesses provided. A medication called prednisone, which doctors often prescribed for elderly patients suffering from chronic arthritis, provided just one example.

Prednisone could promise no cure for arthritis—there was no known substance that could do more than ease the pain caused by this ailment that afflicted so many aging persons.

Yet, because prednisone relieved the pain more effectively than many other substances, it had come into wide use since its introduction in 1955. The usual dose doctors prescribed was three tablets daily. Sold under the brand name of one of the leading drug companies, these tablets cost thirty cents apiece, so the average patient's bill for prednisone would come to about a dollar a day, or thirty dollars a month.

It took no expert witness to explain that many of those who suffered from arthritis were retired people living on their Social Security payments. At the then current rate of these payments, their monthly bill for prednisone could easily take half their total income. Toward the end of each month a large number of these people were having to choose between buying food or taking pills to ease their pain.

But it was further testimony that provided the real shock. Although prednisone had only recently been developed, some small laboratories that were not owned by any of the leading drug companies were selling it, in wholesale quantities, for as little as *two cents a pill.*

Why, then, did the leading companies in the field charge druggists a wholesale price of nearly *eighteen cents* a tablet?

And, if cheaper prednisone was available, why did so many doctors specify the particular brand name of the expensive tablets when they wrote prescriptions for their patients?

In his attempts to get answers for these questions, Senator Kefauver kept feeling as if he were sinking into some sort of quicksand. No matter how many times he asked officials of the drug companies concerned to justify their pricing policy, the only reply he could elicit was some bland statement that did not really provide any information.

"The best indication that our prices are not excessive and that our products are good is found in the ready acceptance given to them by the medical profession," one company's president said.

When pressed to say whether it did not strike him as unjust that poor and elderly people were having to pay so much for their prednisone, he answered: "Undoubtedly some people find it difficult to pay for needed medication. They will also have some difficulty in meeting their rent and food bills as well. It seems to me that this question must be viewed in its true light—it is a matter of inadequate income rather than excessive prices. . . . It is not limited to aged people. It is just plain inability to pay for the necessities of life, where income has not kept step with today's cost of living. I suggest that a citizens' advisory committee be created to work with welfare representatives and your Congressional staffs, so that businessmen from the so-called basic industries like food, housing, and drugs can offer their assistance in resolving their social problem. We are doing this for the underprivileged and underdeveloped countries—why not help our own underdeveloped people? Needless to say, if I personally could be of any help in this way, I would be only too happy to do so."

Senator Kefauver could only shake his head. How could he cut through this fog of words to make it clear that drug companies must develop a new attitude? He was positive that prednisone was merely one instance of the way the industry was taking unfair advantage of the American public. In the case of other drugs where the holder of the patent rights refused to let any competitor use his formula, except on payment of high licensing fees, there was obviously another sort of agreement, because the prices charged by the so-called competitor were usually identical almost to the penny. The consumer had no chance at all of finding a bargain, as was just barely possible in the case of prednisone.

By hammering away steadily at hearing after hearing,

Kefauver gradually learned quite a lot about the drug industry. He concluded that it was particularly susceptible to monopolistic control for several reasons, particularly that it had a "captive" market. Not only did the eventual buyer of its products almost always lack the knowledge to decide what medicine might help him, he had to depend on his doctor to write a prescription before he could make a purchase.

The result was that the person who paid the bill had practically no say about what he was buying, while a small group of middlemen—the nation's physicians—had a great deal of power. And in a natural effort to win friends among these middlemen, the drug industry had come to focus its advertising and other promotional efforts on this small community.

Under a constant barrage of free samples, while the merits of all kinds of new drugs were being advertised in every medical journal, many doctors naturally tended to prescribe products made by companies that had proved their reliability in the past.

Yet there was another factor that struck Kefauver as the crux of the matter.

The terrible toll of injuries during World War II had propelled medical researchers to make unprecedented advances, and new "miracle drugs" were being introduced every year or two. At least 90 per cent of the prescriptions being written called for medicines unknown twenty years earlier.

This undoubted boon to humanity also had its negative aspects, Kefauver soon decided. For the United States was one of the few countries where the discovery of a new healing formula could be protected by a patent and marketed for the exclusive profit of the patent holder. And the patent system not only encouraged drug companies to keep on introducing "new" products, even though these might not be any more effective than products already on the market, but it also gave each company a great incentive to bombard doctors with advertising making extravagant claims for the new product. Furthermore, the expense of all this advertising created a sort of vicious circle. Because the companies spent so much money on promotion efforts, they felt justified in charging ever higher prices—and when they were criticized for setting such high prices, they pointed out that they had already used large sums on the advertising campaign necessary to launch a new product successfully.

Drug-industry spokesmen who appeared before the Kefauver committee did indeed base part of their defense on the high cost of winning acceptance for a new product. They made even more of a point, though, about the costly research programs they were supporting, which in the long run were certainly a great benefit to all humanity because so many advances in medical science had come from them.

Nevertheless, Senator Kefauver kept probing for precise figures about costs and profits, and finally he got sufficient financial data to arrive at a general conclusion. Since 1957, the drug industry's profits had averaged around 20 per cent of its total investment, while the comparable figure for manufacturing as a whole was only around 10 per cent. "In plain language," the senator said, "the drug industry is charging all the traffic will bear."

It was able to do so because the major companies had such a large share of the total market and also because they did not really compete against each other in any meaningful way, other witnesses said. Even when they were selling identical products, they rarely engaged in the conventional form of competition—cutting prices. Instead, they developed a new kind of gimmick.

"The pharmaceutical industry does things differently," a professor of pharmacy explained. "They use two sets of brand names. One consists of the name of the company, such as Lederle, Pfizer, and so forth. In addition, they add a second brand name by inventing a new name for the product and registering it as a private trademark."

Suppose, he went on, that Heinz and Campbell and other makers of baked beans used a similar naming system. "They would all stop using the word 'beans,'" he explained, "and each would give the product a new coined name. Some might use anagrams of beans, like 'Sneabs,' or 'Nabes,' and others might call them 'Lo Cals' or 'Hi Pros.' Picture the confusion in the grocery store if beans were no longer named beans, but if each maker gave a completely new name to his product. Further, try to imagine what would happen if there were three hundred to five hundred additional new names of this type in the grocery store every year."

That was just about what was happening in medicine, he said, and even doctors were becoming increasingly confused.

However, neither Senator Kefauver with all his hearings nor President Kennedy with his special message was able to move the Congress as a whole to take any action affecting the drug industry. It took a doctor named Frances Kelsey to provide the decisive push.

Dr. Kelsey, the mother of two teenage daughters, had only recently moved to the Washington area when her physician husband accepted a research post at one of the government-sponsored National Institutes of Health. She had practiced medicine and taught medical students back in South Dakota, so she began looking for some interesting work of her own as soon as her family was settled in its new home. The job she found was with the Food and Drug Administration, and her first assignment put her on the road to fame.

It seemed like a perfectly routine task. Under the provisions of existing regulations, the drug industry was supposed to seek FDA approval before putting any new medicine on the market. The agency's powers in this area were rather vague, though, and if an application was supported by some evidence that the drug appeared to be safe, the usual practice was to approve it within sixty days. Thus, when a reputable Cincinnati company asked permission to start selling a new tranquilizer that was already being widely used in West Germany and England, there appeared to be no reason for Dr. Kelsey to hesitate.

The new drug was called thalidomide, and its West German discoverers made some remarkable claims for it. They said it was not only a highly effective tension-reliever but also the best and safest cure for sleeplessness that had yet been found. It was also being used in cough medicines and for asthmatics, and to ease the nausea that frequently upset pregnant women during the early months of their pregnancy. The most remarkable claim of all was that it had no unpleasant side effects which might limit its usefulness.

But Dr. Kelsey had seen something in the first reports about thalidomide that made her ask the company for more research data. Why did it seem that the drug had a different effect on animals than on humans? Strangely enough, it did not appear to make animals sleepy, and she wondered if the reason for this might be that the medicine was being absorbed into their systems to cause some future complications.

While she was waiting for the Cincinnati company to submit the results of various animal tests she requested, Dr. Kelsey read a letter in a British medical journal that aroused her suspicions further. The letter was written by a doctor who had been prescribing thalidomide for many patients, and he said he had noted a surprising number of instances in which the patients complained of numbness in their feet and fingers. Could this be caused by the thalidomide? More seriously, the numbness did not subside after the patients stopped taking thalidomide. The condition seemed to be permanent.

At the same time, while Dr. Kelsey kept infuriating officials of the Cincinnati company by asking for more and more research reports, some doctors in West Germany noted that a particularly pitiful kind of birth defect was appearing in many newborn infants. The defect, in medical terminology, was called "phocomelia," from the Greek words *phōkē*, meaning "seal," and *melos,* meaning "limb." In plain language, the victims of this rare abnormality had an arm or leg missing, with only a short stub resembling the flippers of a seal.

Suddenly phocomelia was no longer a rarity in West Germany. Eight clinics which had not seen a single case during the years between 1954 and 1958 had twelve cases in 1959. And then in 1960, eighty-three cases. And in 1961, 302 cases.

Even more horrifying, these cases were not the typical kind that had occurred from time to time in the past. Instead of having only one arm or one leg deformed, as had been reported most often in medical literature, the victims of this terrible outbreak were almost all missing three or even four limbs.

Late in 1961, a Hamburg doctor finally stumbled on a clue. The mothers of several of these infants had been taking thalidomide before the birth of their babies. Late in November, the German Ministry of Health issued a warning to all physicians that the drug was suspected of being an important factor in causing phocomelia.

Yet it took another five months for the connection to be definitely established. In Europe, too, drugs were often sold under a confusing assortment of brand names, so that some mothers and even some doctors were not aware that a particular bottle of pills prescribed during the early period of a woman's pregnancy had, in fact, contained thalidomide. At last, though, the conclusion became inescapable. In every recent case of phocomelia—in England and Scotland, as well as in West Germany—the "harmless" thalidomide had caused the gruesomely crippling birth defect.

During all these months, the Cincinnati company had been pleading with Dr. Kelsey to let it begin the extensive selling campaign it had planned. Large sums of money had already been spent for licensing fees and for preliminary publicity. The company president and his top aides kept making trips to Washington to complain that they were suffering financial hardship. "They came in droves," Dr. Kelsey noted dryly a few months later.

As far as the company officials were concerned, Dr. Kelsey was a stubborn and unreasonable woman—a prime example of the "stupidity" shown by minor government officials when faced with a simple business problem. Yet Dr. Kelsey's superiors—and her physician husband—backed her in her insistence that research on this new drug's safety was still "incomplete in many respects."

Even so, and without violating any existing law, the American company was already distributing thousands of sample packages of thalidomide, under its own trade name of Kevadon. These went to doctors all over the country, who were told that the drug would soon be cleared for use in treating numerous ailments. How many pills were actually given to patients on an experimental basis nobody could say for sure.

But in March of 1962, after receiving reports from Europe that thalidomide had been taken off the market, the American company quietly withdrew its application for FDA approval. It also asked doctors to destroy their free samples, but again nobody could really know what happened to all the Kevadon. Not a word about the whole episode reached the general public until July 15, when the Washington *Post* printed a story giving the first account of Dr. Kelsey's long delaying action. It credited her with having prevented the birth of thousands of deformed babies.

Overnight Dr. Kelsey became a heroine. Senator Kefauver stood up in the Senate to praise her "courage and devotion to the public interest." President Kennedy invited her to the White House and, while her husband and daughters looked on proudly, he presented her with a medal for distinguished public service, then used the occasion to do some more "lobbying" on behalf of the nation's consumers. He said the thalidomide case proved beyond any doubt that a strong new law, such as the one Senator Kefauver was sponsoring, was needed to protect Americans against some similar tragedy in the future.

The majority of Americans agreed with him. Despite a last-ditch fight by industry spokesmen, Congress finally passed Senator Kefauver's measure in October of 1962. Then President Kennedy asked Dr. Kelsey to attend another ceremony at the White House, and she and Senator Kefauver both watched him put his signature on the bill.

Again, this new law was neither as strong as its sponsors had hoped nor as weak as the drug industry had tried to make it. Under its terms, the Food and Drug Administration was given extensive new authority to regulate the introduction of new drugs on the American market, and also a variety of other powers designed to prevent the industry from over-charging or confusing prescription buyers. How effectively the measure would be enforced could not be predicted, and yet consumer leaders felt more optimistic than they would have just a few years earlier.

7

One *Million?*

About twenty miles northeast of Times Square, in a rundown factory district in suburban Mount Vernon, an old brick plant where optical lenses used to be ground casts a long shadow across a narrow side street. By the beginning of the 1960's, this rather forbidding-looking building was bringing light to more than half a million people all over the country.

Behind its grimy walls, engineers and technicians with a talent for rigging up strange and wonderful testing machines had made much of the interior into a series of laboratories. The rest of the space was a maze of cubbyhole offices for writers and editors—and subscription clerks. This was the headquarters of Consumers Union, from which hundreds of thousands of copies of the magazine *Consumer Reports* were mailed out every month.

The main business here was still careful research into the relative merits of different brands of clothes washers or lawn mowers, and the publication of the results among the largest possible readership. But Consumers Union had taken on another function, too. With the increasing general interest in the consumer movement—and in the absence of any one figure who could speak for the whole movement—*Consumer*

Reports had come to be accepted as the most important single voice representing this newly popular cause.

The original Consumers' Research group founded by F. J. Schlink was still functioning in the small New Jersey town of Washington, and Schlink still directed its operations, but somehow it had never won as wide an influence as its Mount Vernon offshoot. For the time being, this New York suburb was, in effect, the national capital of consumerism. The editors who produced *Consumer Reports* every month had given Senator Kefauver the strongest and most unwavering backing he had had from any direction—not excluding the White House —throughout his fight to win stricter regulation of the drug industry. The magazine carried such weight for one simple reason: its circulation was bounding upward.

From a plateau of around 100,000 during World War II, the readership had started growing as soon as peace came. By 1952, the total number of subscribers reached 500,000— and kept right on climbing. At the same time, a barrier that had previously kept the magazine from using the standard circulation-building tool of advertising in other publications began melting away. Instead of turning down ads for *Consumer Reports* with the excuse that major advertisers would object if this gadfly magazine was assisted in any way, advertising departments of newspapers and other magazines now let it be known that they had changed their policy. Since times were changing, they were willing to print ads for *Consumer Reports*.

The sacks of incoming mail arriving at the old factory building got heavier and heavier. The circulation manager spoke up hesitantly. Wouldn't it be wise, he asked, to start making plans for distributing a million copies every month?

One *million*? In the foreseeable future? That would put *Consumer Reports* among the small company of magazines with mass appeal. But why not! The same alert minds that had taken this monthly out of the dull and humorless category of the typical "do-good" publication began to make plans to double—and then redouble—their facilities.*

Meanwhile, the letters-to-the-editor column on the second page presented a seemingly endless flow of specific complaints or requests for additional information, each with its own brisk caption provided by the editors: DAMAGE FROM DRAIN CLEANERS, or POPPED PINS, or THE EGG IN THE NOG. The section entitled "Quote without comment" contained a new collection every month of eyebrow-raising remarks made by businessmen. For instance, there was the statement by a prominent psychologist hired to advise the makers of men's socks:

> Men must be made to feel that discarding the old unworn sock is a masculine, aggressive, executive decision, not a feminine trait. . . . The sock user should be reminded that while he has a close attachment to his sock, *he doesn't love all of them equally.*

This advice had originally appeared in a trade journal under the title, "Soxology: A Strategy for Stimulating Sock Sales." It was by monitoring such publications ordinarily seen only by the people who worked in a particular industry that the editors of *Consumer Reports* found some of the most startling material for the magazine. The hard-hitting comments the consumer editors wrote themselves did even more to establish the monthly as required reading for anyone deeply interested in consumer trends.

After the fight for a new drug law was won, the magazine

---

* By the early 1970's the magazine's circulation topped the two-million mark.

turned its main attention to Senator Douglas's Truth-in-Lending bill and Senator Hart's Truth-in-Packaging bill. Besides attacking businessmen who were trying to defeat both these reforms, the magazine also criticized public officials severely when they did not live up to the standards of wholehearted devotion to consumerism.

It charged that President Kennedy's "Consumer Bill of Rights" and his Consumer Advisory Council were merely window dressing which made a good first impression but did not signify much. After Lyndon Johnson took over the White House, he, too, received much caustic comment when he made a bid for consumer support.

"For too long the consumer has had too little voice and too little weight in government," President Johnson said. "Now that situation is changing. The consumer is moving forward." And he announced he was forming a new high-level Committee on Consumer Interests headed by his own special assistant on consumer affairs, Mrs. Esther Peterson. A former assistant secretary of labor, Mrs. Peterson got the consumer magazine's stamp of approval as an able and forceful advocate. However, the President himself got a much lower mark because he had given Mrs. Peterson so little real power.

The right way to cope with the problem had been pointed out by Senator Kefauver back in 1957, *Consumer Reports* asserted. Then he had introduced a bill to create a new Department of the Consumer, under the direction of a secretary with the same rank as all the other members of the President's cabinet. Not only would this new department be given full charge of the varied consumer-related programs scattered throughout the executive branch of the government, but it also would have the duty of defending consumer interests at every level of government policy-making.

This pioneering effort by Senator Kefauver won scant support, but with some modifications he presented it again at every new session of Congress. Within a few years, he had made enough headway to get twenty-three other senators to join him in sponsoring the measure. After his death in 1963, Senator Kefauver's plan was kept alive by some of these colleagues, but they fared hardly any better than he had. Even the majority of *Consumer Reports* readers couldn't be convinced to demand action on this issue.

Nevertheless, there could be no doubt that the magazine exerted a great influence on public opinion—an influence extending even beyond the increasing ranks of its own subscribers. People who shrugged off the notion that they were consumers were still attracted by a chance to save money. In addition, the old idea that any criticism of American industry was "un-American" no longer carried very much weight. By the middle of the 1960's, a good many citizens suspected that American industry was putting too much stress on making profits and paying too little heed to the public interest.

Most particularly, there was a new concern about the role of industry in polluting the environment. Products of every description now seemed less solidly made than they used to be, and this widespread deterioration in quality disturbed even some conservative-minded people who had once put all consumer spokesmen into the category of dangerous radicals. For all of these reasons, *Consumer Reports* had become a powerful force in its own special field of endeavor.

Its impartial ratings of dozens of different categories of consumer products won it a rare degree of loyalty. When it said that Brand D of dishwasher gave the best value of any brand on the market, including several with much higher price tags, retail sales of Brand D shot upward. When it reported that Brand R of frozen orange juice struck a taste panel as the nearest approximation to fresh juice, some wise

Wall Street investors hurried to buy shares in the company that put out Brand R.

On the other hand, if the magazine said a particular scouring powder contained a substance so abrasive that it could permanently mar the porcelain of kitchen sinks, Mount Vernon might be the scene of an irate confrontation. Waving a copy of the offending issue, some top executive of the company that made the frowned-upon product might furiously demand an apology in the next issue. Under the mistaken belief that nobody had any right to print unfavorable comments about a particular product, the angry manufacturer often threatened to start a lawsuit. But gradually the magazine's reputation for fairness grew to the point where many of these scenes took on a different tone.

Then the manufacturer would politely request detailed data supporting the low rating. Soon afterward he would return to announce that he had ordered various steps to be taken to correct the defects, and he would demand equal publicity about the improved product. If the new claims proved to be justified, a note to this effect did appear in a subsequent issue.

But some manufacturers went even further in demonstrating how much they had come to value the magazine's opinions. On receiving a high rating, they were so impressed that they wanted to reprint the kind words from *Consumer Reports* in their own advertising to attract new customers—ignoring the notice in every issue that forbid such use of the test results. Then it was the editors who not only threatened to start a lawsuit but actually started—and won—several court actions.

For the foundation stone on which the magazine rested was its strict policy of avoiding the slightest tie with any business interest. To preserve complete independence had been one of the basic aims set forth back in 1936 by its parent group when it first began operating. The parent group—Consumers Union, usually called CU in the magazine's pages—still supervised the program. Every subscriber to the magazine was technically a CU member, but for all practical purposes the CU board of directors and the staff that put out *Consumer Reports* were in charge of policy-making. And one of their principal goals was always to keep the magazine above suspicion.

Every product tested was bought and paid for by CU shoppers who took great pains to make themselves appear as ordinary purchasers in case a retailer or manufacturer be tempted to offer free samples or take some other step in the hope of getting a more favorable rating. Purchases were made in widely separated neighborhoods, for instance, and often in different parts of the country. Items too bulky to be carried away easily were delivered to dummy addresses or the homes of staff members, rather than directly to the Mount Vernon headquarters.

But it was at headquarters that ingenuity really flowered. How could an engineer tell if the bars of a baby crib would stand constant rattling by a determined infant? Did a manufacturer have a sound basis for claiming that the fabric used for his ski jackets would wash spotlessly clean no matter what spilled on it? Did cats prefer some particular brand of pet food?

To answer countless questions like these—to provide scientific methods for evaluating new products every month— the *Consumer Reports* staff had been forced to devise a rare collection of special tools. Some looked weird, others merely mysterious. Anyone privileged to tour the magazine's laboratories was almost certain to emerge dazed by the experience.

Your first stop might be a large chamber containing twenty

or thirty sparkling new baby cribs. The bright glow of fluorescent lighting fixtures suspended from the old factory ceiling and the neat rows of empty cribs give the scene an unreal quality, like a stage setting. This effect is heightened by a peculiar sort of robot that has been suspended from the ceiling. It appears to be made out of pieces from a child's erector set and it has a heavy weight attached to one arm. At the sight of this odd hammer hanging overhead, you involuntarily draw back and your guide smiles.

"It's perfectly safe," he says. "We've had lots of practice rigging up testing devices with erector-set parts. This one is going to let us find out if a crib mattress can take constant bouncing when a youngster learns to stand up and jump. Even if we did want to use live babies for this test, it wouldn't make sense because we couldn't be sure they'd be consistent in their efforts—that is, if they'd jump just as hard each time. But the weight will drop down on each mattress with a specific force at measured intervals—it's a forty-pound weight, by the way, because our people have found that's about the most a baby will weigh before he's moved into a bigger bed."

Moving then with your guide, you enter another large room obviously devoted to testing sporting goods. Tennis balls are lined up on a shelf beside a machine with fierce-looking jaws that subjects each ball to precise amounts of pressure, while an attached dial provides a reading measuring minute changes in the ball's surface. In addition, there is a tumbling machine that can simulate the wear and tear of actual play on a concrete or an asphalt court. A third machine drops each ball repeatedly, at the same time producing a tape that gives precise data measuring the ball's liveliness.

In another corner of the same room, a different sort of test is in progress, this one involving clothing for the sports

fan. Ski jackets of assorted styles and hues are being mechani-
cally pulled and tugged to simulate actual wear. Later on,
they will be dabbed with the contents of four different bottles
to see how stain-resistant each jacket really is. One bottle
contains coffee, the next mustard, then ketchup, then "standard soil," the latter being a product manufactured only by
Consumer Reports. Although it looks rather like shoe polish,
it is actually a carefully measured mixture of a lot of common staining agents. By using it for a variety of tests, technicians can draw more accurate conclusions about a fabric's
soil resistance than would be possible if they used other
products whose composition may vary slightly.

Next you might stop to inspect some of the numerous areas
devoted to tests involving food. Freezers and refrigerators
line the walls here, there are stoves for cooking, and little
booths for tasting. Most of the tasters are staff members who
look forward not to have to bring their lunch to work every
few weeks, but they never know in advance what they will
be eating. To prevent even unconscious bias, they never
know the name of the particular brand of ham or cherry pie
they are sampling, either. As is the general practice on every
sort of test, elaborate coding systems are used to keep the
staff in the dark about the origin of each item being tested.
Another routine procedure with food as well as with many
other items is to conduct additional tests under actual household conditions. Most of the homes are those of CU employees, but in many different phases of the testing operations,
outside assistance is also enlisted.

In the case of cat food, for instance, four hundred cats
were brought to Mount Vernon, and they spent a few months
eating and being minutely observed in one of the consumer
laboratories. Then, after doing their part for scientific inquiry,
the cats were shipped to a South American country on an-

other sort of mission. Their services were requested to help control an alarming increase in the local rat population.

Yet by far the most attention-getting of the magazine's tests cannot be seen in Mount Vernon but in rural Connecticut. There, on a special course, the strong and the weak points of every category of car are investigated for an annual spring automobile issue—and by the mid-1960's, the results had become unquestionably the biggest attraction among all the regular features that appear in *Consumer Reports*. Because the average family spends more money for its automobile than for any other purchase it makes, with the exception of its home, the readership of the April guide surpasses any other monthly issue.

When even non-subscribers are thinking about buying a car, they often borrow a copy of the magazine from a friend or from a library. And not only does the April issue reach more readers, it also has the strongest impact on the readers. As the national toll of auto-accident deaths and injuries keeps mounting, the magazine's harsh comments about Detroit's failure to put any significant effort into designing safer cars arouse increasing anger among consumers.

Nevertheless, *Consumer Reports* cannot seem to make its force felt in Detroit, no matter how strongly it condemns the auto industry for stressing styling features above safety factors.

Then suddenly a new voice does reach Detroit—in 1965. And that year marks the real start of the Consumer Revolution.

8

Enter Nader

"When are you going to run for President?" a student asked.

The thin, dark-haired, intense young man on the platform had just finished making a speech, and the question period was starting. This first query brought a roar of cheering from the college audience. It took quite a while for it to subside.

"I find I am less and less interested in who is going to become President," Ralph Nader finally replied. "A far more interesting question is, who is going to become president of General Motors?"

Then cheers and laughter erupted again. Humor—and human interest—had at last enlivened a solemn subject. After more than half a century of ups and downs with only an occasional brief period of drama, the cause of consumerism had found a hero. And a villain, too. In a real-life re-enactment of the old Bible story of David and Goliath, a seemingly hopeless contest between one young lawyer and the mighty General Motors Corporation had captivated the American public.

Ralph Nader's struggle with the giant corporation was so obviously a new version of a familiar old story that writers went back to Biblical language when they tried to explain

its implications. For instance, a pamphlet prepared by the
Public Affairs Council assessed the Nader impact this way:

> And it came to pass that to that land of fiery creatures
> which was called Detroiticus there came an advocate. Of
> little fame, but of great determination was he. And he
> spake unto the Council of the Greats saying unto them,
> "For ye have loosed upon the land a plague of Things,
> and these Things do maim and even kill my brethren,
> and these Things ye have called Corvairs. Yea, though
> ye are great and I am humble, I do call upon ye to re-
> move this plague from the land. And this call I make
> for the Kingdom of Consumers."
>
> And the advocate, he called Nader, returned to the
> capital city where he caused to be written new laws;
> laws which would aid and comfort his people, the Con-
> sumers. Thus did he show the way for the Not So Greats,
> those called Consumers, to petition their Supreme Lead-
> ers to act against the Greats whose Things do foul the
> airs and waters, and who take toll in exchange for their
> fruits of the lemon tree.
>
> Many of the Not So Greats joined together under the
> banner of the advocate, and they became known across
> the land as Nader's Raiders. And the Raiders did study
> the laws, and found they were good, and they said,
> "Let us use these good laws for the betterment of our
> brethren, the Consumers." And unto the Council of the
> Greats they said, "Beware, for upon you is visited the
> Age of the Consumer."

Nader's own story started in Winsted, Connecticut, where
his parents settled after emigrating from Lebanon. Ralph,

one of four children, was born in Winsted on February 27, 1934.

Throughout his childhood, his parents made a point of discussing public affairs at the family dinner table. Sometimes the discussions went on long after dessert was finished, with each member of the family expected to take part. Ralph's father always urged the children to stand up for their rights. "Never kowtow," he would say. Looking back years later, Nader remembered that these sessions had given him a strong sense of justice and civic duty.

By the age of eight, Ralph had already been in the courthouse in Winsted listening to lawyers argue cases. His own mind was made up before he finished high school—he would become a lawyer, but a different kind of lawyer, one who defended the people.

At Princeton, Ralph began to develop the independence that marked him later on. Scornful of the conformity of his fellow students, he refused among other things to wear the white buckskin shoes that were part of the undergraduate uniform at Princeton then. More important, he was offended by the rigidity of the curriculum and he took what he considered to be the most flexible courses. Some of his most deeply enjoyable hours were spent in the campus libraries and he had a true scholar's love for Chinese and Oriental studies, in which he majored.

Nader graduated in 1955 with high honors and entered Harvard Law School, where he soon demonstrated a concern for his fellow students. Angered by what he felt was the arbitrary power of the college administration to expel students without the right of appeal, he tried to interest his classmates in the issue of due process for students. But they were not interested—yet.

While he was still studying law, Nader began to give special

attention to a new subject—automobile safety. He spent
many hours doing research into court cases arising from auto
crashes, and became convinced that the law unjustly put all
the blame for crashes on drivers, while letting the makers of
faulty cars escape penalty. As editor of the Harvard Law
School *Record,* he wrote an article for the student journal,
headlined "Cars Designed for Death"—an article that was
to shape his future.

After graduating and serving six-months active duty in the
Army Reserves, Nader went into private law practice in
Hartford, the capital of Connecticut and the home of some
of the country's biggest insurance companies. Still angry
about unsafe cars, and insurance policies and laws that
seemed combined against the best interests of the driving
public, he continued his research into auto accidents. He
wrote articles, made speeches, and appeared before committees of the state legislature. But he made no progress toward
changing the law. In 1964, at the age of thirty, he decided to
go to Washington.

"I had watched years go by and nothing happened," he
explained later. "I decided that what it took was total com-
bat."

But neither Washington nor the nation knew that war
against unsafe cars had been declared. Nader, a lanky six-
footer who wore gray suits that always seemed a little too
big for him, was, and is, a shy man. He took a room in a
boardinghouse and avoided the social life in the capital. At
first, he worked as a consultant for the Department of Labor,
writing a report on what the government should do about
auto safety. It took him about a year to discover that he was
not making any impression on the government bureaucracy.
He quit his job in early 1965 and began writing a book to
alert the general public to the problem of auto safety.

His very first sentence set the angry tone of the book: "For more than half a century, the automobile has brought death, injury and the most inestimable sorrow and deprivation to millions of people."

He noted that a Department of Commerce report had estimated that 51,000 persons would be killed by automobiles in 1975, but the rate had increased so fast that the projected figure was being reached a decade ahead of schedule.

Working furiously in his room in Washington, taking time out only to eat in restaurants and buy bags of cookies to munch on, Nader busied himself with analyzing facts and figures about auto accidents. He interrupted his work only to furnish material to a Senate committee that had started to investigate auto safety.

Around him were some slight signs that people were becoming more concerned about the causes and prevention of auto accidents. Senator Abraham A. Ribicoff, who had made a national reputation by cracking down on speeders while he was governor of Nader's home state of Connecticut, had opened hearings on what he called the "fantastic carnage" on the highways. Senator Gaylord Nelson of Wisconsin introduced a bill to regulate tire safety. Senator Warren Magnuson of Washington said he would hold hearings on safety, too.

At a Senate hearing in early 1965, the president of General Motors, James M. Roche, took the witness stand. He defended his company's policy of making safety features optional equipment on cars, available only if customers wanted to pay extra for them. For years, the auto industry had taken the position that customers wouldn't buy safety. "If we were to force on people things they are not prepared to buy, we would face a customer revolt," another executive had said.

The whole industry appeared to be positive that the American people wanted bigger cars with more horsepower and more speed. People were buying these cars in record-breaking numbers, then driving them on new superhighways, and the accidents mounted. But auto manufacturers answered their critics by repeating that driver education was the solution to auto safety problems.

That answer did not stop the critics or satisfy consumers. Foreign cars with less horsepower sold more and more. Citizens' groups organized in many areas to fight additional superhighways. Consumer and auto magazines openly discussed defects in American cars, and legislators began to ask pointed questions of the auto makers.

During the 1965 hearings, Senator Robert F. Kennedy leaned forward and interrupted Roche, who had just testified that GM had given a million dollars to the Massachusetts Institute of Technology for collision research.

"What was the profit of General Motors last year?" Senator Kennedy asked.

Roche started to reply. "I don't think that has anything to do . . ."

"I would like that figure, if I may," Senator Kennedy insisted.

After consulting some of his aides, Roche finally answered that GM had made a profit of $1.7 billion during the preceding year.

"And you spent one million on safety?" Kennedy said. "If you gave just one per cent of your profits, that is $17 million," he concluded, sitting back to signify he had no further questions at the moment.

The implications of Kennedy's line of inquiry were clear to the public. It certainly seemed that General Motors and the other auto companies were, in effect, ignoring safety.

Then, when Nader's book called *Unsafe at Any Speed* came
out later that year, citing dozens of cases where safety in
cars had been sacrificed for design, the public was outraged.
The book made front-page news around the country.

In it Nader cited cases where brakes, tires, and visibility
were downgraded to make cars look better and sell better.
He accused the auto industry, the engineering profession,
government agencies, and traffic-safety organizations of failing the public. His point was that if some crashes were
inevitable, cars should be designed to protect the passengers
within them.

"In fact, the gigantic costs of the highway carnage in this
country support a service industry," he wrote. "A vast array
of services—medical, police, administrative, legal, insurance,
automotive repair and funeral—stand equipped to handle the
direct and indirect consequences of auto injuries.

"Traffic accidents create economic demands for these
services running into billions of dollars. It is in the post-
accident response that lawyers and physicians and other
specialists labor. This is where the remuneration lies and this
is where the talent and energies go.

"Consequently our society has an intricate organization to
handle direct and indirect aftermaths of collisions, but the
true mark of a humane society must be what it does about
prevention of accident injuries, not the cleaning up of them
afterward."

Nader went on to charge that General Motors, the nation's
largest manufacturer of autos, had committed "one of the
greatest acts of industrial irresponsibility in the present century" by putting the new Corvair on the market in 1959.
Presenting a case history of how design had triumphed over
safety in the production of this car, Nader described the
Corvair as exceptionally dangerous, with a built-in instability

and a tendency to roll over. He mentioned a rising number of lawsuits against the company from Corvair buyers.

General Motors reacted by deciding to investigate its critic. Lawyers for the company said they felt that Nader was a mystery man and wanted to find out whether he was connected with any of the lawsuits being filed against the company. There were other people, however, who felt that GM was trying to discredit Nader personally.

Nader first realized he was being followed. Then he began to receive bothersome telephone calls at his boardinghouse, despite the fact that he had an unlisted telephone number.

"Mr. Nader?" a voice would inquire.

"Yes."

"Cut it out! Cut it out!" the mysterious voice would say.

Then the connection would be broken, but soon the telephone would ring again. On the night of February 9, 1966, while Nader was working on a statement to be read to Senator Ribicoff's committee on auto safety the next day, he received six anonymous telephone calls.

Soon afterward, a private detective even questioned Nader's former classmate at Harvard who had been paralyzed in an auto accident and to whom Nader had dedicated *Unsafe at Any Speed*. The investigator asked first about Nader's political beliefs and whether his Lebanese ancestry had made him anti-Semitic. He also wanted to know why Nader wasn't married.

The detective also seemed to be interested in Nader's driving habits. He wanted to know whether Nader had a driver's license and whether his friend had ever seen Nader driving a car.

Nader himself was approached, too. In Washington, while he was in a drugstore leafing through an automobile magazine, a young woman walked up to him. She apologized for being forward, then asked him if he would like to take part in a foreign affairs discussion in her apartment. He politely declined.

Several days later, when Nader was in a supermarket, another young woman approached. She asked him if he would come to her apartment and help her move some heavy furniture. Suspicious, Nader refused. He noted that she left the store without asking anyone else to help, although there were other men there.

In March of 1966, newspapers began to print stories about the investigation of Ralph Nader—and they made him famous. For Nader insisted that the giant auto industry was trying in this way to silence him, and the mere possibility that such a big industry was using these soap-opera tactics against a single individual fascinated the American public.

At first, the auto industry called the charges ridiculous. "You can bet that if one of us was doing it, it would be a lot smoother," an industry spokesman said. "If we were checking up on Nader, he'd never know about it."

General Motors, Nader's chief target, also denied that it had taken part in any such investigation. Then Roche received a telephone call from the corporation's legal department. He heard for the first time that one of his aides actually had ordered this inquiry into Nader's background.

So on March 22, 1966, Roche appeared before Senator Ribicoff's committee on auto safety and apologized to Ralph Nader. He admitted that the corporation's private-eye harassment tactics had been "most unworthy of American business."

So the outcome of the episode was exactly the opposite of what General Motors had intended. Instead of discrediting Ralph Nader, the company made him a hero. And all the publicity the incident stirred also assured passage of the Motor Vehicle Safety Act of 1966, which established a new government agency to set mandatory safety standards for cars and trucks.

In still another by-product of this melodrama, Nader sued General Motors for invasion of privacy and settled out of court for $425,000. He used the money, along with his lecture fees and royalties from his book, to form what he called the Public Interest Research Group, his own nonprofit law firm.

Even more important for the future of the consumer movement, though, within a few months Nader had become the idol of countless students around the country. Some of them followed him to Washington to work with him on his investigations of government and business. They shared his passion for hard work, long hours, and low pay. Soon a newspaper dubbed them "Nader's Raiders," and the label stuck. With Nader's help, they put out almost a dozen books during the next several years, examining many different aspects of governmental and business activity. By 1971, they and he were chiefly responsible for the passage of at least six major laws.

Although Nader no longer works alone, he still puts in about a hundred hours a week, more than twice the time the average man or woman spends on the job. He has little time for social life.

"Does the desire to bowl or to play bridge never come to you?" a television interviewer once asked him.

"I don't differentiate between work and recreation," Nader replied. Then he added rather severely, "I'm not saying that people shouldn't enjoy recreational facilities, but I think that the more leisure you see in this country the more it seems to be wasted. People watching professional football games, they used to watch them five hours, now ten, now fifteen, and pretty soon it'll be a thirty-hour endeavor. And there are just other important things to do."

If most other people could not match Nader's own example, they did admire his dedicated spirit. More than any other single individual in the country, he was regarded as the outstanding figure in the Consumer Revolution of the late 1960's. For instance, in a 1971 Gallup Poll taken for *Redbook* magazine of 137 graduating law students at twenty top law schools, Nader was "the most admired" on a list of names that included the finest and most important lawyers and judges in the country.

Despite this widespread recognition, Nader showed no political ambitions and brushed aside suggestions that he ought to run for office. Instead, he spent his spare time traveling to college campuses everywhere. He encouraged students to prove their commitment to his cause by doing more than merely applauding him. He asked them to contribute money to develop a fund that would recruit lawyers and other experts who could defend consumers throughout the country.

"Suppose students would engage in one of history's greatest acts of sacrifice and go without soft drinks, tobacco, candies and sweets, on which they spend about $250 a year per student on the average," he would say time after time. "They could develop the most powerful lobby in the country."

9

Catching Up

Students were undoubtedly the largest and the most effective new group Nader attracted to the consumer cause. At almost every campus, and especially at law schools, admirers of Nader formed committees loosely allied with him but pursuing their own special objectives. With each passing year, more and more high-school students got involved in the consumer movement. So did housewives and working women. And so did increasing numbers of men.

For it was not the least of Nader's accomplishments that he changed the public image of "the consumer." An important obstacle to the growth of consumerism had been the unpleasant associations most people had for the term. Besides being stingy and suspicious, the typical consumer had been assumed to be female—and, as increasingly vocal women's liberationists were now pointing out, any quality commonly thought of as feminine tended to be less well regarded than a masculine trait, not only by most men but by many women, too.

Thus, Nader's own image had an important bearing on the movement's sudden growth. By his success in battling a giant, he changed almost everybody's mental picture of the typical consumer. Now it was clear that a consumer was a person who was willing to go on fighting despite great odds—and America had always had a soft spot in its heart for the underdog. That the most widely publicized consumer advocate in history was a forceful young man helped even more. Others, including many who disliked what Nader stood for, could hardly avoid admiring his quick mind and his capacity for hard work.

Apart from the intangible matter of giving the consumer movement a wider appeal, Nader's chief contribution was easier to measure. He did not invent consumerism, and he was by no means the only figure responsible for turning a diffused reformist impulse into a mass movement so powerful that experienced political leaders called it a revolution. Still, in the five years after Nader first made headlines in 1965, consumer triumphs began coming thick and fast.

Besides the Motor Vehicle Safety Act of 1966, there were also laws setting new federal standards for coal mining and for natural-gas pipelines. Regulations for inspection of meat and poultry products were made stricter, and so were the rules about radiation emissions from electronic devices.

In the same period, the two long-pending "Truth" bills were finally adopted, too—Truth-in-Lending and Truth-in-Packaging. Neither these nor any other protective law, however, passed without last-ditch opposition from business interests. Right down to the final vote on each proposal, spokesmen for various trade associations repeated variations on a single theme: "Sponsors of this legislation have no faith in the American system of competitive free enterprise."

Nevertheless, the tide in favor of increasing consumer protections had become stronger, and even a good many businessmen were willing to concede the need for federal action. Diehard opponents of restrictions on package sizes still wrote magazine articles with titles such as "Let's Keep Politics out of the Pantry," contending that the American housewife liked being able to choose among a multitude of different sizes and shapes of breakfast cereal boxes and that her freedom of choice would be undermined if any sort of rules were enforced. But *Advertising Age,* a trade paper, wrote frankly:

> There are a good many things about governmental probes that we don't like, and we have the continuing feeling that the investigators can do better with their time and energies in most instances, than by fooling around with relatively minor points in marketing or advertising.
>
> Yet we must confess that, as consumers, our sympathy lies with the statements of Senator Hart's subcommittee which concern deception, and particularly deceptive packaging. It would be nicer, we think, to live in a simple world in which "pound" packages contained 16 ounces, and not 15 or even 14½; in which "quart" bottles were actually quarts, not fifths, or even maybe 25 ounces; in which packages containing the same weight or volume didn't look as though one were twice as big as another . . .

So it was hardly surprising when Senator Hart finally got his packaging measure passed in October 1966. It was not surprising, either, that *Consumer Reports* took only a mildly enthusiastic tone in commenting about the victory. Considering the vigorous campaign that manufacturers had been carrying on for five years to avoid compulsory standards regulating package sizes, the compromise provisions giving industry a year to work out voluntary standards were probably the best that could be expected, the magazine said. Nevertheless, even though the new law was "short of what it should be," the passage of any version still had to be hailed as "something of a legislative miracle."

Repeatedly during this period, the same mixture of disappointment and triumph greeted new legislation. One after another, protective measures that were neither as strong as consumer leaders wanted nor as weak as industry opponents tried to make them kept emerging with the approval of both houses of Congress. A health warning on cigarette packages, stricter licensing for clinical laboratories—the list of health and safety protections, as well as regulations, making the federal government a referee in many buying and selling transactions, grew longer and longer.

Among the new areas that came under official scrutiny for the first time were two that had a great emotional appeal. After a fire swept through a home for the elderly when a new type of synthetic carpet burst into flame with terrifying swiftness, a measure establishing flammability standards won passage in Washington. So did a bill designed to keep dangerous toys out of children's hands.

"We're finally catching up!" consumer leaders cheerfully told each other.

But they were well aware that all the new victories were in fact aggravating an old problem—the problem of enforcement. Even with big budget increases, could any federal agency do a really effective job on any of these new programs in a country as large as the United States? And because the responsibility for enforcing consumer protections was divided among so many different agencies of the government, could anything be expected but much talk producing little action?

Consumer advocates who now had more experience in the ways of politics had other questions. Why did so many different bureaus and offices and departments share the task of administering the various protective programs? Was all this cumbersome machinery intended to assure businessmen that they had no reason to worry about being overly hampered by any of the new laws?

Nevertheless, the trend toward giving the consumer a higher rank in Washington could hardly be missed. For it was during the late 1960's that a new stream of reform virtually doubled the force of consumerism. This was the separate but closely related environmental-protection movement inspired by a shy scientist and writer named Rachel Carson.

Her book *Silent Spring,* published in 1962, had raised many troubling questions about the widespread use of DDT and other chemical insect-killers. Some nature lovers and scientists had previously tried to warn their fellow citizens that it was very dangerous to tamper with man's natural environment. But these warnings went largely unheeded until Miss Carson found a way to attract attention.

With a poet's gift for giving simple words a deep meaning, she had started by describing an imaginary town and what happened to it. "There was once a town in the heart of America where all life seemed to live in harmony with its surroundings," she wrote. After briefly picturing the peaceful turn of the seasons, and the magic that had occurred every spring for as long as people could remember, she went on, "Then a strange blight crept over the area and everything began to change." A spring came when no baby chicks hatched. No fish swam in the streams. Along the roadsides, instead of fresh green stems, only brown and withered stalks were to be seen. Above all, no birds sang. Only silence lay over the fields and woods and marsh where a white powder had fallen like snow a few weeks earlier.

"No witchcraft, no enemy action had silenced the rebirth of new life in this stricken world," Rachel Carson wrote. *"The people had done it themselves."*

By presenting a dramatic case against the continued use of chemicals like DDT, Miss Carson aroused great controversy. Some critics accused her of exaggerating the harm that could be done by pesticides, and she was also charged with ignoring the benefits of such chemical agents. Agricultural experts claimed that food crops would be much harder to grow without chemical assistance. Some medical researchers pointed out that spraying malaria-carrying mosquitoes and other insects known to cause fatal diseases had saved many lives. The chemical manufacturing industry mobilized its full resources to fight any efforts to restrict its production.

Yet the public at large believed Miss Carson. She died only two years after her book appeared, yet she lived long enough to blush with dismay when total strangers approached and told her she would go down in history. At the same time, other scientists who had been vainly trying to spread the same message suddenly found a ready audience. Within a few years, a term that had been used only in science texts became one of the most popular words in common usage.

Ecology. The branch of science dealing with the relationships between organisms and their environment had become a much broader subject. Its many aspects were stirring heated debate—not only in classrooms but also in city halls, at business meetings, on street corners. Was it in the public interest to continue to allow the use of washday detergents that seeped into inland waterways, upsetting the balance of nature? Should a new power plant be built if it was bound to spoil an untouched wilderness? How could the air pollution caused by car engines be controlled?

These and similar questions had clear political implications. In almost every case, the public interest in saving the environment collided with the special interest of some particular group. Up until the late 1960's, comparatively few efforts had been made to restrict any private or governmental project on the sole grounds that it would have a negative effect environmentally. Except for the brief period in the early part of the twentieth century when President Theodore Roosevelt and the Progressives had made "conservation" a major objective, the preserving or improving of the nation's natural heritage had excited hardly anybody besides bird watchers and science teachers.

Then almost overnight the whole country began hearing arguments why all sorts of activities should be prevented in the name of ecology. Expanding on the pollution-by-chemistry theme that Rachel Carson had stressed, other people emphasized waste-disposal problems or even the adverse effects of factory noises and odors. The basic point that too many humans were crowding the earth, and thus inevitably causing more pollution of every kind, was hammered home at meetings about "the population explosion."

Political leaders at every governmental level were quick to note the new importance of all this ecological concern. In San Francisco and New Orleans, citizens' committees proved strong enough to stop construction of superhighways that threatened to cut another smog-producing concrete swath through their cities. Similar success rewarded other groups who were also fighting new roads or jetports or factories throughout the country.

As a result, candidates for public office found it increasingly profitable to display an interest in ecology. Then, if they won election, they discovered they had to keep up their interest to retain the loyalty of a great many voters. The impact this had on governmental policy took two different directions.

The most obvious was the creation of a network of environmental-protection agencies which assumed some functions that were being performed by other bodies. These agencies were also charged with a variety of duties that had previously been neglected—from harbor clean-up operations to tulip planting. Towns, counties, cities, states, and the federal government all joined in the effort.

At the same time, the consumer movement benefited, too. In the first place, it was almost impossible to draw a clear line between the areas of specific concern to consumers and those of importance to the ecology-minded, because their interests overlapped so often. Campaigns against chemically tainted food drew support from both camps, as did attempts to regulate industry's growing reliance on elaborate and waste-making packaging. Even more important, though, was the fact that the same fundamental principle motivated both movements: *the public interest ought to take precedence over private profit-making.*

In effect, this was also a fundamental principle of the American form of government, as consumer leaders and ecologists both liked to point out. But they held that over the years the interests of businessmen had been given increasing weight, while the public as a whole had suffered. What they wanted, they said, was merely to restore an old tradition, not to impose a new system. If they kept pressing the government to take on an increasing role, they insisted, it was only because industries had become so powerful that no other umpire could enforce the rules.

"Socialism!" Some businessmen still used this cry as the answer to every demand for new limits on industry. But the combined strength of the two other movements could not be ignored by elected officials. Even the conservative-minded Richard Nixon appointed a special assistant to advise him on consumer problems soon after he entered the White House in 1968.

And a new attitude became apparent even among many of the industrialists who had fought the hardest against new measures proposed by consumer advocates. In the old days of machine politics, when men like Boss Tweed had been threatened with a reformist uprising, they had coined a slogan. "If you can't beat 'em, join 'em."

The Consumer Revolution brought a sort of modern updating to that old slogan.

10

"If you can't beat 'em . . ."

Even Ralph Nader never claimed that America's business community had no good qualities. When he lost his temper at a Senate hearing, after being accused of not giving the auto industry any credit for its great achievements, he still admitted—at least indirectly—that 90 per cent of the time its behavior was respectable. Yet his generally critical attitude, echoed by many of his followers, had far more impact than the occasional words of praise consumer leaders uttered about businessmen.

The most obvious result of this lack of balance between praise and blame was a defensive reaction on the part of industry and its friends. For instance, President Nixon's Secretary of Commerce, Maurice Stans, noted:

> The American economy did not grow to a trillion-dollar gross national product—with nearly two-thirds of it going to consumers—through the schemes of the male-factors, and the quick-buck artists, who represent nothing more than a tiny fringe of the business community.

The main result, though, was an unprecedented amount of soul-searching by industry leaders. Never before had business spent so much time, energy, and money in examining itself, its products, its advertising, and its public image. Under the pressure of mounting consumer discontent and increasing government intervention, responsible businessmen began taking numerous steps to adjust to the situation confronting them.

Thoughtful executives stood up at one meeting after another to say that much of the consumer dissatisfaction had come about because of advertising that promised more than the product could deliver. These speakers repeatedly stressed that consumer anger arose when a product did not perform satisfactorily. They said that the consumer ran to the government for help when he could not get action on his legitimate complaints from any other quarter, and they warned their colleagues that if they wanted to escape more drastic government interference, they would have to bridge the gap between consumer expectation and business performance.

At practically every business convention, the audience was told that it could no longer dismiss its critics as "un-American." Nor could one point to the great majority of satisfied customers, ignoring the discontented. Back in the early 1960's, a leading advertising executive had said, "Stop worrying about every piddling criticism of our business. If there is any collective quality of the public, it is indifference." At the beginning of the 1970's, another major figure in the industry provided a new philosophy for a new decade: "If it is true that 99 per cent of all transactions give full satisfaction to the buyer, then an effort should be directed at isolating the one per cent and seeing that they conform."

The machinery for dealing with dishonesty among their own ranks already existed, in the form of the Better Business Bureaus which had been founded during the first wave of public alarm about advertising excesses. Dating back half a century, this self-policing effort had been undertaken to discourage governmental interference by the new Federal Trade Commission, and also to demonstrate that business could keep its own house in order.

In theory, the Better Business Bureaus were admirable. As far as businessmen were concerned, they showed that industry as a whole stood for responsibility, honesty in claims and dealings, and integrity in the performance of business services. The various local bureaus were supposed to investigate any complaints that arose in their own cities, but they all acted on the assumption that complaints would be few in number and would mainly stem from honest error rather than outright dishonesty. Operating on these assumptions, Better Business Bureau employees used persuasion as their main tool for correction. They also saw no need for setting up large offices or otherwise spending much money. In fact, their budgets were quite limited, since their sole income came from the nominal dues paid by members. Over the years, about a thousand national corporations joined, as did about eight hundred Chambers of Commerce and a number of trade organizations. Altogether they supported 140 Better Business Bureaus around the United States and eleven more in Canada.

But what really happened when a consumer called with a complaint? Listen to these candid appraisals made during the late 1960's by officials of the Better Business Bureaus. One of them said that, in a five-year period, phone calls and other communications handled by BBB offices increased more than 100 per cent and that the Bureaus received seven million requests for assistance, more than all government agencies combined. But, he added, about twice as many more consumers were unable to reach BBB offices with complaints because of lack of facilities, equipment, or personnel.

The chairman of the board of the BBB organization was even more critical.

"Local Bureaus were badly understaffed and limping along on starvation budgets," he said at an agency convention in the late 1960's. "Requests for services were lost in the shuffle of staggering workloads. Many businessmen brushed off the Better Business Bureau as a bunch of ineffectual, idealistic do-gooders. Conversely, critics charged that the Better Business Bureau was an advocate, a protective association, if you will, of big business."

From the consumer's point of view, according to an outside critic of the BBB, the problem was more serious than clogged telephone lines. It was of no help to a consumer, he said, to be told that all three plumbers about whom he inquired had no blemish on their records—if he doesn't know what the BBB means by the word "blemish." This critic cited the following anecdote to show how a more complete inquiry service would help businessmen as well as consumers.

A man in Virginia called his local Better Business Bureau to ask about three auto-transmission-repair shops. The answer was, "They cooperate with us; all of them are okay." He found out later that one of the firms he had asked about had many lawsuits filed against it and had been in trouble repeatedly with the Federal Trade Commission. So the man wrote to one of the other recommended firms: "I don't know if your reputation is any better than that other firm; the Better Business Bureau won't say. If it is, perhaps this letter will have some effect on changing the Bureau's policy of benign neglect. How many of your customers have been assured by the Bureau that the other firm is a good dealer? How many thousands of dollars have *you* lost as a result?"

Late in the 1960's the rising tide of consumerism reached

the inner councils of the Better Business Bureaus. In effect, the BBB itself joined the Consumer Revolution. The first moves took place quietly and behind the scenes.

A committee of vigorous and forward-looking executives was formed to consider ways and means of updating the BBB program, and not unexpectedly it decided that money was badly needed if any meaningful change was to be accomplished. So the committee members fanned out around the country and went right to the presidents of leading corporations. Then they did some polite arm-twisting.

They started by pointing out a statistic the corporation president might have missed. "Did you know," the BBB emissary would say, "that the number of people in this country who think all advertising is a batch of lies has gone up from 20 per cent fifteen years ago to just about 50 per cent of the entire population?" So, of every dollar spent for advertising, about fifty cents was being wasted, and this figure might climb even higher unless some drastic action was taken to restore the average American's faith. But how could this be done? The BBB man was ready with a specific suggestion.

"We want you to reallocate your marketing dollar where it will do some good toward cleaning up the marketplace. So we suggest that you give us one-quarter of one per cent of your national advertising budget to improve the effectiveness of the remaining 99 per cent."

In practically every case, the corporation president would say, "That makes sense to me."

Then out would come pencils and pads, and the results of some simple computations might make the president have sudden second thoughts. For the advertising budgets of major corporations had risen to the point where the specified quarter of one per cent might turn out to be $600,000—compared with the token contribution of $3,000 the same company had given the BBB the preceding year.

Yet the high-level BBB fund-raisers were sufficiently persuasive to win over most of the business leaders they approached, and within a few months the BBB had an unprecedented war chest. Then a broad-scale expansion and reorganization began. Under the direction of a new Council of Better Business Bureaus, steps were taken toward five basic goals:

1. To upgrade and improve the operations of local BBB offices; for instance, by installing two and a half million dollars' worth of new telephone equipment and hiring new people to man it.

2. To develop effective new programs for consumer education, with special kits for school use, and to develop innovations like turning buses into mobile information stations traveling from shopping center to shopping center.

3. To set up a consumer-data center in Denver where, by means of a computer, information about products and complaints could be stored and immediately consulted by BBB offices everywhere, whenever a consumer inquiry called for making comparisons.

4. To sponsor a stronger code for voluntary self-regulation of advertising on a national and not merely a local basis.

5. To establish mediation or arbitration panels to handle consumer complaints that went beyond the scope of local BBB offices, providing an effective machinery for settling consumer grievances without clogging the courts with lawsuits.

As a general statement of its new stress on pleasing consumers, the Council of Better Business Bureaus also issued a new set of guidelines for its members, which it called the Ten Commandments for Business. These were:

1. To assume full personal responsibility for the quality and performance of the product or service I sell. The responsibility extends to every phase of my business, from research and development through design and manufacture, to sales and service.

2. To recognize that consumerism is not a passing fad or a figment of the politician's imagination, but a genuine rising tide of dissatisfaction, disillusionment, and indignation by consumers.

3. To build money's worth into my product.

4. To be honest in my advertising. Not simply to stay within the Federal Trade Commission's tolerances, but to start with a sincere intention to inform rather than deceive. To charm, beguile, and entertain the consumer with my advertising, to add beauty and gaiety to his life with my packaging and promotion—but not to fool him.

5. To avoid—in sales contracts, labels, and promotional efforts—making promises that will not be delivered, or even creating expectations that are not likely to be fulfilled.

6. To institute consumer service departments if none already exists. To open lines of communication with my customers and respond rapidly to their complaints.

7. To cooperate with standards or practices established by my industry association.

8. To devote more of my total marketing dollars to the consumer.

9. To channel a proportionate share of those consumer-earmarked marketing dollars through the most effective mechanism for dealing directly with the consumer.
10. To eliminate duplication and overlap, to prevent proliferation in the consumer movement. To counter the hostile voice of consumer advocates with a single, powerful, and positive voice speaking on behalf of business.

It remains to be seen, of course, whether the Ten Commandments for Business will be honored by businessmen and whether consumers will benefit. Even while conceding that self-regulation has not worked too well in the past, spokesmen for business interests continue to argue that self-regulation is better than government regulation. Many consumer spokesmen and government officials dispute that. According to them, it is one of the responsibilities of government to play the role of referee in cases of outright fraud, to guarantee a fair choice of products, to set minimum standards of quality on products that affect health and safety, and, in general, to act for the individual consumer.

However, many businessmen continue to see the expanding role of government as a threat to individual enterprise and to the free enterprise system. *Business Week,* a publication devoted to promoting the interests of businessmen, has reported that in most cases the first reaction of business to legislation aimed at resolving a legitimate consumer complaint is to deny that the problem exists. Only when the proposed legislation is about to become law is the problem admitted, and action is finally taken by business to resolve the problem.

"Is this a credible posture for business?" asked Mrs. Virginia Knauer, President Nixon's special assistant for consumer affairs, at a meeting of top business leaders in Virginia in 1970. She had been invited to speak on "Consumerism— The Problem and Its Solutions" by businessmen who were obviously worried about the growing threat to them posed by the consumer movement.

Speaking in almost motherly terms, Mrs. Knauer pointed out that individual consumers, acting alone, had found it difficult to counteract "the forces of corporate impersonalization, of corporate indifference, of computerized form letters, of being shuttled from retailer to distributor to manufacturer and back again." Is it any wonder, she asked, if consumers look to their government for other solutions?

The Consumer Revolution was a challenge to business to live up to its full potential, Mrs. Knauer said, for its object was to motivate business toward quality, "to give consumers what is promised." Toward that end, she went on, business had "to be honest, to give people a product that will work and that is reasonably safe, to respond effectively to legitimate complaints, to provide information concerning the relevant quality characteristics of a product, to take into consideration the ecological and environmental ramifications of a company decision, and to return to the basic principle upon which so much of our nation's business was structured— 'Satisfaction guaranteed, or your money back.' "

Mrs. Knauer's formula was strong medicine, but there were some businessmen who understood what she meant— they would have to do all those things to satisfy their consumers, or the government would do it for them. They realized that times had changed, that they could not ignore either individual consumers or the organized armies of consumers that were battering at their doors. If businesses intended to survive, they had better join the consumer movement. One of the leading spokesmen for this point of view was

Elisha Gray II, chairman of the board of the Whirlpool Corporation and also chairman of the Council of Better Business Bureaus.

"Business institutions, like individuals, are tested by adversity," he said. "The price of survival is nothing less than accommodation to new social forces." In other words, business had to adjust to the Consumer Revolution—or else face the same fate that had befallen the dinosaur.

11

Hot Dogs and Cherry Pie

Ever since Dr. Wiley's day, there had been shrewd business-men who saw the advantage of making friends in the federal bureaus that enforced the new laws affecting their industries. Instead of fighting with these officials, the businessmen cooperated with them—and the results pleased almost every-body.

Manufacturers who were willing to accept most of the new rules without a murmur usually found that when they did have a complaint, it received a sympathetic hearing. By adopting some basic standards of purity and fair practice, which actually helped most producers because the standards protected them against unscrupulous competition, the leading men and women in many industries were all but assured of having their own point of view respected by the very people in charge of regulating them.

As far as most of the federal officeholders themselves were concerned, this system had several attractions, not the least of them being that it made their jobs much easier. For the task of policing any big industry, even if a large enough staff of inspectors and research experts and lawyers could be coaxed out of Congress, was nearly hopeless in a vast country like the United States. Practically every regulatory agency

114

therefore tended to arrive at a basic policy the Food and Drug Administration described as "preventive enforcement." In outlining this policy, the FDA said:

> First, FDA uses every possible means to make sure that industry knows the full requirement of the law. Correspondence, conferences, speeches, publications, exhibits, and individual counseling are all used by the FDA to inform manufacturers and shippers.

Only after exhausting all such educational efforts would the agency have to consider the harsh step of seizing an offending product or starting court action. Then the repercussions might be unpleasant in various ways. Whether the case was won or lost, ill will was bound to be stirred up, irate protests would probably be lodged by congressmen and other influential figures who had some political reason to defend a particular producer, and the zealous prosecutor might even find himself fired or forced to resign.

It was hardly surprising, under the circumstances, that over the years a rather close relationship developed between the regulators and the regulated. They attended the same conventions, they came to look at many questions from the same viewpoint. If government employees were ever criticized for being overly friendly with businessmen, they justified themselves by pointing out that they were really saving the taxpayers a lot of money. "In this way violations are kept at a minimum," the FDA said. "Most firms want to comply with the law and feel it is good business."

But consumer leaders were less than happy about the failure to develop vigorous enforcement programs. They were even more distressed by the increasing tendency of the FDA and other agencies to look kindly at suggestions from industry sources. As the force of consumerism mounted, so did protests charging various agencies with being much too lax in protecting the public.

One after another, several of the major regulatory agencies became the target of hard-hitting indictments prepared by teams of Nader's Raiders. These students spent months probing for facts showing how each government body was helping profit-hungry businessmen while the ordinary citizen suffered. The Federal Trade Commission, the Interstate Commerce Commission, and the Food and Drug Administration all felt the blast of Raider fire in books which attracted many readers, especially on college campuses. The books "combined exhaustive research with brilliant theater," a *New York Times* reviewer noted. "Where once we could only glimpse occasional skeletons in unrelated closets, Nader has thrown open the entire catacombs." Yet a somewhat ridiculous uproar about one of the staple items in the American diet did even more to educate the general public. This was the case of the U.S. *vs.* the hot dog.

It all started with a routine notice in the Federal Register, where pending actions by government agencies are listed. Appearing during the final months of Lyndon Johnson's administration, the few lines indicated that various revisions of the Department of Agriculture's regulations governing the ingredients permitted in frankfurters were under consideration, and invited interested parties to submit testimony within sixty days regarding the proposed changes. Under ordinary procedure, the witnesses who turned up would be heard at a public hearing, then shortly thereafter a new ruling would be issued in the name of the Secretary of Agriculture. Only rarely did the ruling differ to any marked extent from the original proposal.

But sixty days came and went, and no frankfurter hearing

was held. The fact that President Johnson left office in this interval, and President Nixon took over the White House, might have had some bearing on the delay, for the outgoing Chief Executive was a Democrat and the new one was a Republican, bound to replace many Johnson appointees with those of his own political philosophy. However, a question remained. Could the contents of hot dogs be a matter of any real political importance?

Yes! The answer was not long in coming out into the open. Within a few months, a great frankfurter debate was agitating the nation.

The new Republican Secretary of Agriculture seemed to disapprove of one aspect of his predecessor's proposal—the portion that would give official sanction for including ground-up poultry parts in hot dogs without any requirement that the product's label list chicken or turkey among the ingredients. A Republican-written notice in the Federal Register during the spring of 1969 did not mention this aspect of the original proposal, despite heavy pressure from the poultry industry.

A trade association representing chicken growers was putting on a major campaign to win this point. Hurt seriously by a drop in egg consumption resulting from medical reports citing egg yolks as a dangerous food for people with a tendency toward heart disease, the industry was trying hard to find new uses for its products. Machines had recently been developed to remove the bones from wing tips and other poultry parts that had often been wasted in the past, and a ready market for this cheap form of protein had been discovered among makers of hot dogs and sausages of various descriptions. Now the poultry industry was outraged by the prospect of having this new market closed to it.

Chicken was being discriminated against, the poultry council complained bitterly. "When President Lincoln established the Department of Agriculture a hundred years ago, he called it "a people's department,' " one of its statements said. "We don't recall that he exempted the people who produce chickens."

At the same time, congressmen representing chicken-producing states kept rising to speak on the subject. One Maryland legislator sponsored a "chicken hot-dog feast" in a caucus room so that all his colleagues could taste how delicious the new product was.

But if the Republican-led Department of Agriculture appeared to oppose the poultry portion of the Democratic plan, there was bipartisan agreement on the rest of it. Like their predecessors, the Republican officeholders could see no reason why hot-dog makers should be kept from doing what had recently become customary in the industry. Besides ground meat and flavorings, most hot dogs now contained at least a third of their weight in fat.

There had always been a certain amount of fat mixed with the meat in frankfurters. It was supposed to improve their flavor and texture. But for a good many years the fat content of hot dogs had been more or less stabilized at around 19 per cent—until a "technological breakthrough" during the 1950's.

Then new machinery was developed in Germany which made it possible to mix fat and meat globules so thoroughly that the fat did not separate out during the cooking process. A grilled frankfurter would no longer shrivel to the extent that its fat had melted, and no telltale pool of fat remained on the grill. Always seeking ways to improve their product, American manufacturers soon imported the new German machines.

But instead of using them to mix just 19 per cent fat with the meat in their frankfurters, some manufacturers got the idea of increasing the fat content. Fat was much cheaper than meat, and the costs of doing business were constantly rising. Why not add extra fat, rather than risk antagonizing consumers by charging higher prices?

Then when a few brands took to changing the basic formula—and these were featured in many supermarkets at 59 cents a pound—even the most reputable meat processors felt they had no choice. Their own brands were retailing for 79 cents a pound, or more. Unless they began adding fat, how long would it be before they lost all their customers?

Thus, within ten years, the fat content of the average American hot dog climbed above 30 per cent. Some brands contained as much as 50 per cent fat. Tremors of alarm began to be felt in parts of the industry and in the Department of Agriculture, which was supposed to be protecting consumers in their purchases of meat and poultry. The result was that, by 1968, behind-the-scenes consultation between responsible elements in the industry and their official regulators had evolved the plan published in the Federal Register.

As had happened so many times in the past, the proposed new regulation followed the general policy that industry leaders thought would serve their own best interests. Whether they actually wrote the ruling that would set a 33 per cent maximum on the future fat content of frankfurters—or whether government officials wrote it—was a matter of no real importance. One other point provoked the great hot-dog controversy of 1969.

Why had the consumer been ignored?

For as soon as news stories about the proposed ruling reached the public, howls of outrage arose all over the country. No American liked to find out he had been fooled, and practically the whole population had been peacefully eating hot dogs—at ball games, in school lunchrooms, in family kitchens—without even suspecting that more fat and less meat were going into the average frankfurter roll. *Advertising Age* tersely explained why: "Never underestimate the power of mustard."

Other comments were longer and angrier. For instance, the Pennsylvania League for Consumer Protection wrote from Harrisburg to the Department of Agriculture in Washington:

> What's in a hot dog is no joke to our large number of consumer members who expect us to act forcefully to stop heinous trade practices, like production and sale of fat slops cased in cellophane, and labeled food. Our community action and poverty group organization members are especially incensed because their families rely rather heavily on hot dogs as a major source of meat nutrition. . . .

At the same time, a consumer group operating eight cooperative supermarkets in the San Francisco Bay area, serving nearly fifty thousand member families, sent another long and fact-filled letter to the Secretary of Agriculture. It provided a chart comparing the price and the nutritional value of the two most common protein items offered by California school lunch programs. The hamburger described on its chart conformed to the state's own regulation specifying that ground beef could contain no more than 30 per cent fat and could have no additives such as water, cereal or coloring, spices and preservatives. The frankfurters listed would meet the proposed new federal standard, but would still be inferior to ground beef:

	cost per pound	per cent protein	cost per 20 grams of protein
hot dogs	59 cents	11	24 cents
hamburger	59 cents	16	16 cents

Thus the lowest-price hot dogs would cost 50 per cent more than the lowest-price hamburger, from the point of view of the protein nourishment provided. "We believe," the California group wrote, "that most shoppers have no idea that a pound of hot dogs contains substantially less protein than ground beef while costing about the same or more per pound. . . . A maximum of 33 per cent fat in hot dogs is *too high.*"

A clearinghouse had recently been founded where state and local consumer organizations throughout the country could find out about the activities of similar units in other areas, and could pool their strength to work for common goals. This was the Consumer Federation of America, or CFA, which has its headquarters in Washington, D.C. Besides a steadily growing number of new groups devoted exclusively to the consumer cause, the federation's membership also included several large national organizations that were expanding their own programs in the same field. These ranged from various labor unions to the National Board of the YMCA, the National Council of Senior Citizens, and the National Farmers Union.

Whether the CFA could be built into a forceful pressure group on behalf of all consumers remained to be seen, though. Its main asset during the years immediately following its founding in 1967 was a young woman named Erma Angevine, who had covered the Kefauver hearings as a reporter for a chain of regional newspapers. The testimony she listened to day after day had so aroused her own crusading instincts that she had quit journalism to take on the assignment of directing the new federation. Now with an impressive title on her office door, she was busily lobbying for congressional support to oppose the Department of Agriculture's frankfurter plan.

Yet the decisive blow was struck, after all, by a woman who was not only a Republican but also a personal appointee of President Nixon. Making her first official appearance as the President's consumer adviser, Mrs. Virginia Knauer bravely contradicted him. Nixon had recently let it be known that he saw nothing wrong with a 33 per cent fat limit for hot dogs, but right in front of television cameras the sprightly and grandmotherly Mrs. Knauer said 30 per cent was quite enough.

And that's what the Department of Agriculture finally decided, after the President smilingly told a press conference he really didn't blame Mrs. Knauer for taking her new job seriously.

With the USDA's announcement compromising on the 30 per cent figure, most of the frankfurter furor died down. Comparatively little fuss was caused when a separate hearing reconsidered the poultry question. A South Dakota farm wife wrote a furious letter protesting against letting chicken "compete unfairly with red meat products." And another woman wrote to urge the Secretary of Agriculture not to let chicken or turkey be used in hot dogs because "I don't eat feather meat of no kind." Nevertheless, hardly anybody else seemed upset when the Agriculture Department formally decreed that frankfurters could still be so labeled if their meat content included up to 15 per cent poultry.

Although the consumer movement could scarcely claim it had won a victory, the hot-dog controversy did seem to demonstrate that a new stage had been reached. Not merely in the setting of government policy, but in the day-to-day operation of federal agencies, there was less and less likelihood that consumer interests would be forgotten. Some of the most obvious signs of the changing official attitude were to be found at the very agency that had previously been the focal point for consumer critics.

By the start of the 1970's, the Food and Drug Administration had clearly come a long way since its basement beginnings as the Agriculture Department's bureau of chemistry. In the complex scheme of federal organization, it now belonged under the wing of the Department of Health, Education, and Welfare, but all by itself it had more duties than Dr. Wiley could have dreamed of. With the opening of the new decade, it also had its own new building sprawling over several acres of former Maryland farmland, about twenty miles from downtown Washington.

Responding to the increasing pressure from consumers, the agency had swung around onto a new course in many of its programs. Instead of giving industry the benefit of every doubt about the harmfulness of a particular product, it has begun taking the opposite tack. The buyer—and not the seller—is more and more often receiving the benefit of any reasonable doubt.

In a case that got wide publicity, the FDA issued a decisive order banning the family of artificial sweeteners known as cyclamates. Despite the growing popularity of "diet" foods and drinks containing these low-calorie sugar substitutes, the agency ordered manufacturers to stop selling all products using cyclamates. The ruling was not universally applauded. About a billion dollars' worth of canned fruits and drinks containing cyclamates were being bought every year by 1969, and the leaders of this large industry naturally protested at the prospect of having to change their formulas. Some ordinary citizens and also some physicians objected that these products were serving a useful purpose, and that no positive evidence linking cyclamates to cancer had yet been discovered to justify such a drastic step. As for the Nader type of convinced consumer, this camp issued sharp statements condemning the FDA for taking nearly twenty years to do its duty: the first hints of the dangers of cyclamates had turned up as early as 1950.

Yet, though it might seem that nobody was satisfied with the way the agency was doing its job, the chorus of complaints was misleading. One could see that the FDA of the 1970's had shaken itself out of its former inactivity. Its staff and its budget were still much too small to cope with all the various tasks Congress had given it, but now the agency was at least trying to be more forceful.

Since the FDA's main role was to protect the public, its top officials thought the public ought to be kept better informed about the specific programs originating at its Rockville headquarters. Under the terms of existing law, the setting of standards defining the acceptable ingredients in numerous common products occupied many research technicians. Their objective was to guarantee that whenever a shopper bought a jar of mayonnaise or orange drink, the contents would conform to certain basic rules. Only specified ingredients could be used in these standardized products, although the manufacturer still could combine them according to his own recipe. He could also add certain optional ingredients that would have to be listed on the label.

According to dedicated consumers, this was a typical example of a halfway measure that did not give the buyer nearly enough help. For once an official FDA standard was set for any product, its label no longer had to list the basic ingredients set forth in the standard. Consumer leaders thought labels ought to contain more—and not less—information to guide individual shoppers in making their selections. Nevertheless, the prevailing opinion at the FDA itself was that setting industry-wide standards gave the buyer far better protection than any mere labeling requirement could. The official standard describing mayonnaise, for instance, ran to several pages of small print starting:

Mayonnaise is the emulsified semisolid food prepared from edible vegetable oil and one or both of the acidifying ingredients specified in paragraph (b) of this section, and one or more of the egg-yolk-containing ingredients specified in paragraph (c). For the purposes of this section, the term "edible vegetable oil" includes salad oil that may contain not more than 0.125 per cent by weight of oxystearin to inhibit crystalization . . .

And so on for several thousand additional words, listing all permitted seasonings as well as basic ingredients. A comprehensive description like this really helped the consumer much more than any listing of ingredients on a product's label, according to FDA policy makers.

The FDA's public-information program was therefore expanded in several different directions. To show the broad scope of its surveillance over the marketplace, it began issuing "public warnings" whenever a potentially dangerous product was discovered on sale anywhere in the country. It also began to publish a monthly magazine, *FDA Papers,* describing FDA-sponsored experiments—and also listing details about the enforcement action taken by the agency's seventeen regional offices. In a typical issue, seizures and court actions filled eight or ten large pages, under such headings as: DECOMPOSED CANNED TOMATOES or UNAPPROVED DRUGS or ILLEGAL FIREWORKS.

At the same time, new emphasis was put on providing FDA speakers to address public meetings. Educational pamphlets were sent out in increasing quantities, and these not only tried to explain the agency's many operations but also sought to interest students in preparing for careers as food and drug chemists or inspectors.

In addition to all these programs, the agency continued its efforts, too, to win public support for its basic policies on such matters as setting food standards. Not everybody was satisfied, though, by the agency's increasing stress on public relations. Did all this mean that the FDA was really doing more? Or was it merely talking more about itself? One of its own information officers wryly noted recently that the old easygoing attitudes had far from disappeared among the ranks of its staff.

In this instance, a project had indeed been started and pushed to completion. After a long series of studies and consultations, an FDA task force had finally arrived at a standard precisely defining the components of a particular product as follows:

Frozen cherry pie is the food prepared by incorporating in a filling contained in a pastry shell mature, pitted, stemmed cherries that are fresh, frozen, and/or canned. The top of the pie may be open or it may be wholly or partly covered with pastry or other suitable topping. Filling, pastry, and topping components of the food consist of optional ingredients as prescribed by paragraph (b) . . .

And so on, for three pages setting the official United States government policy on such questions as how big a cherry pie has to be before it is a pie and how many cherries a pie must contain.

But the public-relations aide shook her head sadly. "Can you imagine!" she exclaimed. "They went to all this trouble, and then they finally handed me the material to write a news story about it—on the day *after* George Washington's birthday. Two days earlier, and the story would have been used coast to coast. As it was, we got hardly a word mentioned."

12

Where to Go?

If government agencies have a hard time getting their message through to consumers, consumers who want help from the government have an even harder time getting through to the government. During recent years, more and more of them have been writing letters:

> . . . my granddaughter wore this pair of panty hose just once and the run was all the way from heel to top. I am tired of the way people are being cheated.

> . . . then after I got the cassette recorder home and tried it, I found out it won't rewind. Tape is hanging out of it like so much spaghetti.

> . . . I have just opened a can of sliced peaches with a net weight of 1 pound 13 ounces, or approximately 3½ cups, as stated on the label. After draining the peaches, I had 1⅔ cups of syrup and ½ cup of peaches. This has happened before with other products. It is maddening not to get your money's worth and to always feel we are shortchanged. What can be done about this?

These are just a few samples from the top of a pile of mail

that arrived at Virginia Knauer's office in Washington the same morning. One letter was postmarked Alabama, another California, the third Illinois. The floor of the room was covered with stacks of similar letters that had been delivered over the past several months but had not yet been answered because not enough hands were available to cope with the continuing flood.

At meetings and on television, Mrs. Knauer and others like her explain how the federal government is seeking to help people get fair value for their money. As a result, sacks of mail describing individual consumer difficulties inundate government agencies in such quantity that merely opening all the envelopes is a major chore. Replying to their contents is an almost insurmountable task.

When a letter complains of a clear violation of some federal law, it can be referred to the appropriate agency. However, many of the complaints are not specific enough— or important enough—to justify any real action by a unit of the national government. No federal agency could follow through on such a volume of petty complaints without costing the nation's taxpayers fantastic sums.

Thus it is fortunate, from the viewpoint of federal office-holders, that many of the consumer complaints seem to be based more on a general feeling of disgust than on any single grievance. Handwritten or typed, covering page after page of expensive stationery or a single sheet ripped from a cheap notebook, practically every letter echoes the same theme. In the words of a Texas man whose wife never received the bottle of perfume he had picked out—and paid for—after studying a mail-order catalogue: "Three dollars isn't much, but I don't like to be taken."

Responding to this sort of emotional appeal, the mail-room staff in many different agencies has learned to combine a sympathetic tone with some wishful thinking. Leaflets describing various programs designed to protect consumers are often sent out to the letter writers, but these do not really explain how the Texas man is supposed to get back his three dollars. The Federal Trade Commission has responsibility for monitoring mail-order sales—which cause more consumer headaches than anything else except auto defects—and where the sum involved is more substantial, information about the proper procedure for seeking legal aid will be provided. However, the federal government is so big—and the separation of educational and enforcement programs has become so common—that the ordinary consumer who needs help on a less than major problem will almost certainly fare better if he or she aims in another direction.

Better Business Bureaus, as noted previously, are an obvious alternative, and they are being consulted increasingly often with increasingly satisfactory results. But consumer experts have one piece of general advice. "Always try the president of the corporation first," they tell the members of their groups. "It can't hurt, and it may accomplish more than you think, if you write a letter setting forth the facts of your case." For a good many corporate executives have been making serious efforts to improve their public image. Several of the leading auto manufacturers, whose industry has been under steady attack ever since Ralph Nader's emergence on the national scene, have even started urging consumers to let them know whenever an irritating difficulty arises.

"Your Man in Detroit" will take care of it, the Chrysler Corporation advertised widely after appointing a new vice president in charge of consumer complaints. And Ford embarked on a similar campaign, insisting, "We Listen Better."

Nevertheless, complaints about cars continue to be the single largest category in the filing cabinets of most consumer agencies. As in the case of other items from toasters to snow-blowers, many of the problems involve dissatisfaction with repairs and servicing. While manufacturers often promise a great deal in the way of providing repair service, and also give warranties or guarantees pledging free replacement of defective parts during a stated period of time, their performance often fails to live up to the promise. If a producer says his own factory has no responsibility for fixing a particular defect, and if there is no local service outlet that will do the job at a fair price, where can the consumer turn?

To his daily newspaper, in many cities. Or perhaps a local radio station. Since consumers have become increasingly vocal, more and more "Mr. Fix-it's" have been showing up in print or on the air. They do not actually fix any carburetors or clothes washers, but they make it their business to find out—and then report—exactly where the distressed buyer can go for some real help, not just another runaround.

Although the numbers of people whose problems are solved in this manner may not be very impressive, the mere fact that these newspaper columns or radio programs have become so popular points up a sobering truth. Consumer problems have mushroomed to such an extent during recent years that it takes a trained specialist to know how to cope with them. Public officials, too, at every governmental level have been learning the same lesson.

They have learned the hard way, for the urban riots of the late 1960's were far more related to the Consumer Revolution than was immediately realized. Most of the people involved in the consumer movement from Dr. Wiley's day to Ralph Nader's have been well-educated, middle class, and white. Yet as many of these very people realized, it was the educationally deprived and poor-black portion of the population who were suffering the cruelest forms of victimization in their role as consumers. After whole blocks of ghetto stores in many cities went up in smoke, the message that consumer frauds were one of the worst indignities endured by the nation's black citizens finally reached a wider audience.

The resentment blacks felt about the way many store-keepers treated them had been no secret. Malcolm X, in his *Autobiography,* had eloquently recalled his own feelings on first visiting Detroit:

> The furniture store that my brother Wilfred managed was right in the black ghetto of Detroit; I'd better not name the store, if I'm going to tell the way they robbed Negroes.
>
> "Nothing Down" advertisements drew poor Negroes into that store like flypaper. It was a shame, the way they paid three and four times what the furniture had cost, because they could not get credit [elsewhere]. It was the same cheap, gaudy-looking junk that you can see in any of the black ghetto furniture stores today. Fabrics were stapled on the sofas. Imitation "leopard skin" bedspreads, "tiger skin" rugs, such stuff as that. I would see clumsy, work-hardened, calloused hands scrawling and scratching signatures on the contract, agreeing to highway-robbery interest rates in the fine print that never was read. . . .
>
> In all my years in the streets I'd been looking at the exploitation that for the first time I really saw and under-stood. Now I watched brothers entwining themselves in the economic clutches of the white man who went home every night with another bag of the money drained out of the ghetto. I saw that money, instead of helping the black man, was going to help enrich these white mer-chants, who usually lived in an "exclusive" area where

a black man had better not get caught unless he worked there for somebody white.

If anyone doubted such testimony by black leaders, a white professor of sociology at Columbia University, David Caplovitz, conducted a detailed study investigating the buying problems ghetto residents faced. *The Poor Pay More* was the book in which he described the results of his inquiry. As just one example, he cited a shopping survey in New York City showing that a particular brand of portable television set cost $139 in a downtown discount house, but when shoppers of obviously different backgrounds tried to buy the same set in a Lower East Side store, salesmen demonstrated how costly the color of a buyer's skin could be. A white law student was told he could buy the TV set for $125; the price quoted to a Puerto Rican housewife was $139; and a black housewife was asked to pay $200—"a racial price differential of 60 per cent!" the professor noted. He also reported that shopping surveys in Boston, Philadelphia, Chicago, and San Francisco had shown a similar pattern.

Another book, this one by a senator from the state of Washington, expanded on the same theme. It was *The Dark Side of the Marketplace: The Plight of the American Consumer,* which Senator Warren G. Magnuson wrote with Jean Carper after listening to witness after witness testify before the Senate's Interstate Commerce Committee. "Perhaps the most striking revelation to me was how skillfully unscrupulous salesmen prey on the fears and insecurities of the poor," the senator said in his chapter on ghetto practices. "These so-called businessmen shamelessly exploit the poor man's desire for credit; his longing for respect, his fear of losing his job, his home—what little security he has built up—and most of all, his fear of being doomed to eternal poverty. In one of

the most vicious rackets I'm sure has ever been worked anywhere, a company in the District of Columbia in 1966, under
the guise of operating an urban-renewal project, frightened
countless ghetto residents into signing contracts for aluminum
fronts for their houses, at prices as high as $4,000 and
$5,000. The salesmen implied that if they did not 'urban-
renew,' they would be 'urban-removed.' "

But the most decisive statement linking consumer fraud
and ghetto riots came in the report of the special commission
President Johnson appointed to study the causes of the
violent upheavals that shook cities all over the country during
the late 1960's. This commission headed by Illinois Governor
Otto Kerner said:

> Much of the violence in recent civil disorders has
> been directed at stores and other commercial establish-
> ments in disadvantaged Negro areas. . . . The fact that
> most of the merchants who operate stores in almost
> every Negro area are white undoubtedly contributes to
> the conclusion among Negroes that they are exploited by
> white society.
>
> This complex situation can best be understood by
> first considering certain basic facts:
>
> * Various cultural factors generate constant pressure
> on low-income families to buy relatively expensive dur-
> able goods. This pressure comes in part from continuous
> exposure to commercial advertising, especially on tele-
> vision. In January 1967, over 88 per cent of all Negro
> households had TV sets.
>
> * Many poor families have extremely low incomes,
> bad previous credit records, unstable sources of income,
> or other attributes which make it virtually impossible

for them to buy merchandise from established large national or local retail firms. . . .

* Most low-income families are uneducated concerning the nature of credit purchase contracts. . . .

* In most states, the laws governing relations between consumers and merchants in effect offer protection only to informed, sophisticated parties with understanding of each other's rights and obligations.

In this situation, exploitative practices flourish. . . . A special kind of merchant appears to sell goods on terms designed to cover the high costs of doing business in ghetto neighborhoods. Whether they actually gain higher profits, these merchants charge higher prices than those in other parts of the city to cover the greater credit risks and other higher operating costs inherent in neighborhood outlets. . . .

The Kerner Report also noted "significant reasons" for believing that poor ghetto families generally paid higher prices for the food they bought, and received generally lower quality, than was the case in other neighborhoods.

Thus, although the ghetto riots in Detroit, Newark, and other cities were not generally considered consumer revolts, the fact that consumer resentment played an important part in fomenting the uprisings could not be denied since looting of those stores where blacks felt they had been victimized was widespread.

One result of the riots, therefore, was that the strength of the black struggle for social justice reinforced the growing strength of consumerism itself, just as the increasing focus on environmental protection did. So a variety of official programs began paying more attention to the special problems facing disadvantaged consumers.

Recently a whole series of educational materials have been produced to simplify some consumer problems. A purple leaflet headlined "KNOCK, KNOCK" is a typical example. With cartoon drawings and large type to make its message easier to absorb, it advises:

When a stranger knocks on your door, he or she is probably a salesman.

Not all salesmen are honest. Some may try to cheat you.

Be Smart . . .

Be Careful

Remember

1. Merchandise sold door to door is often overpriced and may be poor quality.

2. Take two days to think it over. Any honest salesman will be happy to come back.

3. Compare prices of similar merchandise in stores before you buy from a door to door salesman.

4. Don't sign any papers promising to pay unless you know the total cost. (High interest, credit insurance and other service charges may double the price.)

5. Buy only what you need.

6. Remember—you work hard for your money, make every penny count.

NEVER BE AFRAID TO SAY NO!

In addition to trying to spread simple buying advice among consumers who have had few opportunities for learning, official agencies have also been offering guidance that even the most sophisticated shopper often lacks. As daily life becomes increasingly complicated, the poor and the middle class and the rich alike all need the same sort of helping hand.

The news media, with their consumer specialists, are on the right track, but these experts cannot possibly steer every troubled consumer toward the proper source of help. Nowhere is daily life more complicated than in New York City, and thus it is only fitting that one of the nation's most comprehensive guides for the perplexed consumer has been prepared by the city's own Department of Consumer Affairs.

Where to Go? is its title, and it contains eighteen pages of specific listings, telling where information can be obtained and complaints can be registered about sixty different general categories of consumer concern, from advertising to veterans' affairs. The booklet's index gives the clearest evidence, though, of just how confusing the whole task is. In order to cope with the multitude of difficulties that may beset a consumer in New York, it might be necessary to consult any one or several of the following:

GOVERNMENT AGENCIES

New York City
Consumer Affairs, Dept. of
Environmental Protection Administration
Gas and Electricity, Dept. of
Health, Dept. of
Health and Hospitals Corporation
Highways, Dept. of
Housing and Development Administration
Human Rights, City Commission for
Office of the Aging
Police Department
Veterans' Affairs, Division of

New York State
Agriculture and Markets, Dept. of
Bingo Control Commission
Education Dept.
Health, Dept. of
Human Rights, Division of
Insurance Dept.
Labor, Dept. of
Law, Dept. of
State, Dept. of
Veterans' Affairs, Division of

United States
Agriculture, Dept. of
Federal Trade Commission
Food and Drug Administration
Health, Education and Welfare, Dept. of
Interstate Commerce Commission
National Credit Union Administration
Post Office Dept.
Regional Administration of National Banks
Veterans' Administration

PRIVATE AGENCIES
American Red Cross in Greater New York
Better Business Bureau of Metropolitan New York
Brooklyn Union Gas Co.
Community Council of Greater New York
Consolidated Edison
Cooperative Extension, Cornell University
Institute of Life Insurance

Assuming that a consumer has a problem that *Where to Go?* does not mention specifically, his or her best move, the booklet indicates, would be to get in touch with the agency that publishes it. Expanded in the late 1960's to cover a much broader area than the city's former Department of Markets and Licensing, the Department of Consumer Affairs still has charge of issuing licenses to over a hundred types of businesses, from parking lots to employment agencies. Its inspectors conduct regular surveys to check up on compliance with older rules such as those setting accuracy standards for scales used in food stores, as well as with more recent regulations such as those forbidding deceptive packaging of meat by supermarkets. The agency also has a complaint division which seeks to settle disputes "arising out of the sale of merchandise in the City of New York," and if that duty were not sufficient to keep the staff busy, another division "undertakes the investigation of business practices which are deceptive or fraudulent." But, above all else, the Department is supposed to provide a sort of oasis where distracted consumers can be assured of receiving aid and comfort.

So the phones in its headquarters near City Hall never stop ringing. Along with most other public agencies all over the country, this one suffers from severe budget problems, and a corps of volunteers—mainly students and senior citizens—has been recruited to answer the phones in the large room to which nearly a hundred thousand calls a year have been directed during recent years.

"Good morning. Consumer Affairs," a retired dentist briskly says when his phone buzzes.

"I live in Forest Hills and I have a complaint," a woman tells him. "My mother also wants to make the same complaint. You know these flyers stores send out to list their specials . . ."

As the woman's voice runs on rapidly, the dentist reaches for a sheet of paper headed "Complaint against . . ." and he pencils in the dotted lines while listening to the tale of how a particular bargain listed on a green page of the advertising circular was not yet on sale when this shopper and her mother went to the store, and the manager insisted only the items on the pink page were available this week, even though the first page had printed on it, "Sale Starts Monday, April 25."

After requesting that a copy of the offending circular be mailed to him, the dentist hangs up, shaking his head. "She's one of our regulars," he confides. "I'll bet she calls in at least once a month. But where you really get a feeling of doing some good is when you get someone like the poor lady who was conned into signing a 'lifetime' contract at a dancing school, then was being threatened with all sorts of lawsuits because she stopped paying after she got a knee injury. We actually got some money back for her." But he is obliged to break off his story and pick up his phone again.

"My best case was even better," a housewife sitting across from the dentist puts in proudly. "This man called up to say he was going out of his mind because a computer kept charging him for all sorts of credit-card purchases he'd never made. We not only got it straightened out with an apology from the president of the credit-card company, but a year's free membership for the consumer as well."

Part of the reason why New York City's Department of Consumer Affairs receives so many calls has to do with the diligent efforts of its first commissioner, Bess Myerson. Miss Myerson, Miss America of 1945, had gone on to win even wider fame on her own television program before Mayor John Lindsay gave her a chance to make her political debut. Then she quickly proved that a determined woman with an important job could cause a lot of headlines.

Every week, she found new ways to dramatize the consumer's plight. She testified at hearings on telephone rates, filed lawsuits against gyp artists like the TV "repairmen" who carted away sets and presented a bill for $80 or more, without so much as changing a tube. Having been appointed to her job, and having no plans to run in any election, she did not have to worry about offending any particular group of voters. She spoke freely whenever a microphone was held out in her direction. Some of the headlines she inspired hint at the range of her activities.

CITY STUDY FINDS 0 TO 7% PORK
IN 10 PORK-AND-BEAN PRODUCTS

CONSUMER UNIT PROPOSES
REGULATION OF DISCOUNT ADS

MISS MYERSON BIDS F.T.C.
REGULATE CREDIT CARDS

WHERE WILL BESS MYERSON STRIKE NEXT?

Miss Myerson's freewheeling approach to her job had repercussions in many other parts of the country, as well as in her own city. By starting such a variety of new programs, she raised the question of what the role of city government ought to be in promoting consumer interests. Her own answer was simple. Departments like hers, she said, ought to serve as a "people's lobby."

She was particularly proud of innovations like the "con-sumobile," which rolls into low-income neighborhoods complete with loudspeaker and equipment for recording individual complaints. On board there are also helpful leaflets printed in both Spanish and English, including down-to-earth publications like *How to Sue in Small Claims Court in New York City*. "If you have been hurt or cheated by a person or a store, you can sue in Small Claims Court," the booklet's cover explains. "You do not need a lawyer. The procedure is simple. This book tells you how to do it."

Following New York's leadership in this area, a number of other cities both large and small have been instituting similar programs. For instance, Boston and Columbus, Ohio, have both established new consumer agencies, and Chicago has expanded the powers of its Department of Consumer Sales, Weights and Measures. But even Miss Myerson would admit that a fine line has to be drawn between supporting the legitimate interests of consumers and harassing the business community.

"I'm terribly conscious of the fact that it's easy to flail out and hit everybody," she once told an interviewer. "That's simple, and it's not the way it should be done. It would be terribly unfair. Whenever we've accused a particular area of business of less than ethical conduct, the evidence has been there."

But why not depend more on industry's own programs for self-regulation, such as the expanding Better Business Bureaus?

The bearded young lawyer who served as Miss Myerson's first assistant, and who supervised much of the legal enforcement instituted under her direction, shook his head when asked about self-regulation. "It leaves the best people in industry at the mercy of the worst," he said. "The decent people who would respond can't afford to. It's no more sensible to ask for it in consumerism than in school desegregation."

And his view appears to be widely held. For not only city agencies but also state and federal agencies have been defending consumer interests during recent years with decisive action instead of mere words.

13

The Big Sell

What's wrong with these advertisements?

On the television screen, a glass of milk is shown being magically transformed into a Milky Way candy bar.

The Federal Trade Commission objected on the grounds that all that milk did not go into just one Milky Way. As a result, the manufacturer agreed to stop misrepresenting the quantity and quality of milk used as an ingredient in the candy.

The television screen shows a boy struggling with a breakfast of two eggs, two slices of bacon, and toast. His mother says, "No breakfast will do him any good if he leaves it on the plate." Then she explains that two Toast'ems would provide 100 per cent of the boy's minimum daily requirement of vitamins and iron.

The Federal Trade Commission objected, and the General Foods Corporation agreed to stop claiming that Toast'ems were a nutritionally sound substitute for any meal consisting of identified foods, unless it was literally true.

In another television commercial, a young woman in a baseball uniform holds up a bag of Domino sugar and says, "Hey, everybody! You want your kids to have strength,

*energy, stamina, don't you? You need sugar—and not any
old sugar you never heard of."*

The Federal Trade Commission objected. It wanted the
company to stop advertising that the consumption of sugar
was necessary or essential for an active life.

In these cases and hundreds more, the Federal Trade
Commission is acting for consumers by monitoring advertisements to make sure they are not deceptive or misleading.
Established in 1914 to police unfair methods of competition,
the Commission was a not very energetic arm of the government, moving only against the most outrageous cases of
deception, until the late 1960's.

What happened to transform the FTC from a tame cat
with no claws into a tiger fighting for the consumer? Basically,
it was the change in the country—the Consumer Revolution.
But two reports triggered the transformation. The first was a
1969 study by a group of Nader's Raiders sharply criticizing
the agency for failing to do its proper job. Later that same
year, President Nixon asked the American Bar Association
to look into the matter. The ABA's study confirmed many
of Nader's charges and recommended a complete shake-up
of the regulatory body. President Nixon responded by appointing the man who had made the bar association report,
Miles W. Kirkpatrick as the new head of the FTC. In effect,
the President said, "Do it yourself." Then the new chairman
brought in a new staff with a new viewpoint. As expressed by
Kirkpatrick, "It is the Commission's determination to look
to the day when the consumer's market basket is filled wholly
on the basis of price, quality and over-all competitive merit,
and not as a result of discriminatory practices, noncompeti-
tive market structures, or false and misleading advertising.
The consumer movement and the Federal Trade Commission
are both committed to this goal."

The words were brave, but brave words had been heard before in the consumer movement with no marked results. The difference this time seemed to be that the Commission meant what it said. In the months that followed, the agency stepped up its activities against fraud of all kinds, it changed its definition of what was acceptable and what was not, it increased its publications of advice to consumers, and it also invited individual consumers to come in and be heard.

In the background was a major concern about advertising, its techniques and its role in American life. Advertising was big business, it was the lifeblood of the communications industry, it paid the bills that made it possible for modern newspapers, magazines, television, and radio to survive and prosper. It informed people about products, and it often amused them, too. But critics said that advertising often confused people and created a false sense of values.

Consumers Union, one of advertising's major critics, reported, "In 1936, just under $15 per person was spent on advertising persuasion; by 1957, this had risen to just over $60, and by 1970, advertising expenditure had reached $100 for every man, woman and child in the United States. Total expenditures are equally depressing. In 1936, some $1.9 billion was spent to advertise retail goods and services; by 1970, this figure had skyrocketed to $20 billion."

Nobody disputed the figures, but Consumers Union went on to use them as the basis for an opinion that advertising men objected to strenuously. "Every penny of [this money] went into the prices consumers paid," CU said. "All too often, they were paying for false and irrelevant promises. Rarely did consumers get the information usable for product-by-product value comparisons."

Does advertising try to sell people things they do not want? Does it persuade people to want the wrong things? Is it largely uninformative? And does it play on the emotions of consumers?

Critics of advertising said it did all those things, and more. Ralph Nader, for example, said, "Madison Avenue is engaged in an epidemic campaign of marketing fraud." Another critic asked, "How could the consumer possibly function rationally when he is told 1,600 times a day in an endless assault upon all his senses that all products are wonderful, all are best, and why doesn't he buy, buy, buy, BUY?"

This picture of the helpless consumer was disputed by many in industry. They claimed that the housewife was still the queen of the marketplace, that she might be fooled once, but not very often, that her purchasing habits for her family were what determined the marketplace. As one cereal manufacturer put it, the American housewife is a shrewd shopper, and when it came to clever buying, "she could give lessons to a Yankee horse trader." Manufacturers cited examples of products backed by big advertising campaigns that failed, as in the case of the Edsel car. The Ford Motor Company spent over a quarter of a billion dollars in two years trying to sell its new Edsel, but customers just didn't buy. Didn't that prove the customer was all-powerful, these defenders asked.

The answer from the public, the press, and government agencies, particularly the Federal Trade Commission, was, resoundingly, no! Despite all the efforts of advertisers and advertising men to prove that the American economy, with its boast of the highest standard of living in the world, was dependent on advertising, more and more people were questioning the way in which advertising did its job. Almost everybody agreed that advertising was a good way of informing the public about new products, even of persuading people to buy one product instead of another. The dispute came on the matter of how advertising did its job.

The chairman of the board of one of the nation's biggest advertising agencies attempted to answer this criticism at a convention. He asked, "Just how much of a mess is advertising in?" Then he proceeded to answer:

"Ask an advertising man like me and he is likely to say, with all sincerity, that the vast proportion of national advertising is truthful . . . that the small percentage of misleading advertising is mostly local, prepared locally. Secondhand auto deals—that sort of thing. On the subject of taste, he is likely to admit that there are some violations here—inevitably by the other fellow, of course. He is also likely to say that the self-appointed arbiters of taste have different standards of taste from the public at large. And there is considerable truth in what the adman says."

But this adman was frank enough to admit that the public had a different impression. He conceded that never before had advertising and market practices been held in such low regard by the consumer, and he had figures to prove the point. In 1965, answering the question "Which of these statements best describes your feelings about advertising?" 88 per cent of the women interviewed found advertising either "very helpful" or "necessary." Only 10 per cent found it "not at all helpful" or "mostly lies." Five years later, in 1970, only 49 per cent found advertising "very helpful" or "necessary," and exactly 49 per cent found it "not at all helpful" or "mostly lies," while presumably only 2 per cent of those surveyed had no strong opinions on the subject.

Despite these figures, this particular spokesman still held that there was no evidence that consumers believed individual ads less than they had in the past. After all, he said, the survey measured theory, not behavior. But what did businessmen and advertisers really think about advertising when they were not making speeches to the public or defending themselves? They seemed to agree that advertising was essential to business, that it speeded the development of new products and helped to raise the American standard of living. They also pointed with pride toward the nonprofit campaigns some advertisers sponsored to support worthy causes of various kinds. Nevertheless, many were quite uncomfortable at the thought of advertising's power of persuasion, and their own personal opinions about the truthfulness of advertising were quite close to those of the general public.

A survey by the *Harvard Business Review* showed that 85 per cent of the businessmen interviewed by the publication thought advertising persuaded people to buy things they did not need, and 76 per cent regarded this as bad. Back in 1962, more than half of the businessmen interviewed then had believed advertisements presented a true picture of the product advertised. In 1971, that percentage dropped to only 30 per cent. Surprisingly, 60 per cent of the businessmen believed the opposite—that advertisements do not present a true picture of the product advertised.

It was in this atmosphere of growing distrust of advertising and, by extension, business itself, that the Federal Trade Commission started to expand its functions as the public watchdog over advertising and marketing. Invoking previously unused authority, the Commission ordered all major industries to substantiate their advertising claims. If someone says a candy bar "tastes great," we won't ask them for verification, but if they say a car "stops three times as fast," we will ask them for the proof, an FTC official explained.

The first order for substantiation went to seven automobile manufacturers. The FTC ordered Ford to document the claim

that its LTD was "was over 700 per cent quieter," General
Motors to list the "109 advantages" it claimed for the
Chevrolet Chevelle, and Chrysler to document assertions that
the Plymouth Satellite was "America's lowest-priced two-
door sedan." The FTC also asked manufacturers of Volks-
wagens, Datsuns, and Toyotas for their evidence.

When the answers came in, they gave a fascinating look
into advertising techniques. General Motors listed an auto-
matic choke, a body by Fisher, a foot-operated parking brake,
fifteen exterior colors, and classically simple new grilles as
among the "109 advantages" of the Chevelle. Ford reported
that sound meters indicated an average difference of 30
decibels between exterior and interior noises, which trans-
lated in the measurements of sound engineers into eight times
or 700 per cent as quiet inside the car as out. Chrysler listed
the manufacturer's suggested retail price to justify its ads
that the Plymouth Satellite was America's lowest-priced two-
door sedan.

The foreign manufacturers also submitted their own documentation. Volkswagen provided a reproduction of an un-
named technical publication to support its claim that the
Kharmann Ghia "gave up to 26 miles per gallon." Toyota
sent in copies of two of its own test reports to support the
advertisement that the Corolla fastback "gets about 28 miles a
gallon." The Nissen Company of Japan cited factory tests to
justify its contention that the Datsun had "fail-safe" brakes.

In ordering the documentation, the Commission said its
basic aim was to assist consumers in making a rational
choice among competing claims that were supposedly based
on objective evidence. Officials said they hoped advertisers
would be discouraged from making claims they could not
substantiate. If the documentation was not satisfactory, they
said, the Commission would take action to stop the claims.

Stopping exaggerated claims was one thing. But how could the impression false ads made on the consumer be erased after the ads had done their work? The new Federal Trade Commission had an answer for that, too.

Over the anguished pleas of advertisers, it adopted a new concept of corrective advertising. This meant that it was no longer enough for a manufacturer or advertiser to stop his deceptive advertisement. From now on, the advertiser had to inform the public that it had been misinformed—and this in his own ads for the same products. It was as if the advertiser had to apologize publicly for his previous ads.

The very first case under the new doctrine involved bread. The makers of Profile bread had advertised that their bread was less fattening than ordinary bread because it had fewer calories a slice. That was accurate as far as it went. But the ad did not say that Profile was sliced thinner than ordinary bread and, therefore, contained only 58 calories a slice instead of the usual 63. A second claim in the original series of ads was that you could lose weight by eating two slices of Profile bread before every meal. The ad did not say that this would work only if you ate less during the meal. The Federal Trade Commission decided that this was deceptive advertising.

Rather than fight the case in the courts, the ITT-Continental Baking Company, manufacturers of Profile bread, agreed that at least 25 per cent of future advertising for the bread would be aimed at telling consumers that "Profile bread is not effective for weight reduction, contrary to possible interpretations of prior advertising." The Federal Trade Commission had won another victory for the consumer.

Still not satisfied, though, the Commission began a comprehensive study of modern advertising practices, from the ABC's of technique to sophisticated motivational appeals.

Members of the Commission wanted to know more about the way advertisements were created, about emotional appeals to children, and about advertising techniques that implied more than they said.

As might be expected, advertising-industry spokesmen came to the FTC's new series of hearings with varying viewpoints, some defensive, some bitter, some argumentative, but all prepared to cooperate with the agency. They wanted to defend their industry's opinion that advertising was vital to free enterprise, to freedom of choice by consumers, and to the continued existence of a free press.

As an example of the importance of advertising to the press, the chairman of the board of *Time* magazine cited these figures: about two-thirds of magazine and newspaper revenues, or about $7 billion, came from advertising in 1970, while almost 100 per cent of commercial television and radio revenues, or $4.8 billion, were derived from advertising. "Without these revenues, the free press, as it has evolved in America, could not exist," he said.

One leading advertiser presented a bitter view of critics, which was shared by many in the business community. Not only did the current discontent with advertising reflect a distrust of the American system of free enterprise, he said, but distrust of advertising was "taught often and all too well by men whose intentions for our country are either curious or unknown to me."

Yet the idea that criticism of advertising was un-American no longer struck many people as a serious reply. After all, advertising and its practitioners had been fair game for critics for years. Book after book had been written on advertising and its abuses, and Madison Avenue had not fallen apart. More serious were the criticisms that perhaps advertising itself was anti-people, in the sense that it tried to sell consumers things they did not need or want, that it persuaded people to want the wrong things, that it played on the emotions, and that it was largely uninformative.

Defending advertising, one businessman said he had no ax to grind as an advertiser, in choosing any set of appeals instead of another—factual, emotional, or any other. "But I do feel an obligation," he said, "to inform people about what matters to them—that is, the pleasure or enjoyment they can derive from using my product. My commitment is to give the customer what she wants, and if her 'wants' have an emotional component to them, it behooves me to recognize that fact."

He had hit upon the precise point: does advertising give the consumer what he or she wants, or does it create wants that would not have existed without advertising? At the FTC hearings, witnesses answered that advertising could not create demands for unwanted products, and cited numerous examples of products withdrawn from the market for lack of adequate demand.

But the debate raised another point of basic interest: what was the purpose of the economy after all? The conservative view had been summarized by one of the President's economic advisers in these words: "As I understand the economy, its ultimate purpose is to produce more consumer goods. This is the object of everything we are working at—to produce more consumer goods." However, a consumer-minded legislator disputed this view. "The goal of our economy is not the production of more consumer goods at all," he said. "The goal of our economy is to provide an environment in which every American family can have a good house for living and shelter, a good school to which to send the children, good transportation facilities and good opportunities for cultural and spiritual advancement."

Perhaps it was true that business, spurred by advertising, had raised the American standard of living to the highest in the world, with many people—but not all—enjoying more material things than ever before. But the times had changed. Now everybody was a consumer, and consumers were not only questioning the quality of the things they were buying but also questioning whether some of these goods were even necessary. Their message had been heard by politicians in every city and state capital, and especially in Washington. Laws were passed, commissions were set up, consumer advocates were not merely being heard, they were being made part of the government structure. It almost seemed as if the very word consumer was a key to legislative and executive action. Virtually every government agency was climbing on the consumer bandwagon by appointing its own consumer experts.

So the past sins of advertising had caught up with those who were responsible for them. The prevailing opinion in the nation's capital was expressed by a lawyer for the Federal Trade Commission, who said, "The day of the huckster has passed. The American public will no longer accept the proposition that 'all's fair in love and war and advertising,' which seems to have been one of the governing principles of marketing in this country." And even some of the more responsible spokesmen for business, while stoutly maintaining that excessive restrictions on advertising would severely damage our economy and our society, were ready to concede that some regulation was in the public interest.

14

Unfinished Business

Back in a simpler day, people would put a box of newspapers into the foundation of a new building so that future generations could have a few clues to what daily life was like at the time the building was constructed. If this were done at the start of the 1970's, the strongbox would almost certainly contain something about consumers. In this decade, hardly an issue of any major newspaper or magazine failed to mention this topic.

Pick up *U.S. News & World Report,* a weekly aimed at businessmen, and you might discover:

THE RISING ANGER
OVER COSTLY AND SLIPSHOD SERVICES

Everywhere you go, you hear the same story: inferior service at sky-high prices. It's a mounting worry for businessmen as well as their customers.

A tide of consumer complaints is rising across the U.S., overwhelming company executives and Government officials alike.

The complaints tell of soaring prices, defective products, slipshod service, inattentive salesmen. . . . Rarely do people meet for business or social occasions without

launching into "horror stories" about sloppy workmanship or inferior service.

Newspapers make the message even clearer, not only in
their general news columns but throughout their special sections. On the society page of the Washington *Post,* for instance, you might notice:

DECADE OF THE CONSUMER

"The 70's will be the decade of the consumer. People
aren't going to take anymore just what's dished out to
them," said Antonia Uccello, former mayor of Hartford,
Conn., who has been named director of consumer affairs
for the Department of Transportation.

Miss Uccello was received by Mrs. Nixon at a tea
yesterday for the Women's Division of the Sons of Italy.
Miss Uccello is a member of the Hartford lodge.

Miss Uccello described her new job "as being an
advocate for the public on service and goods connected
with transportation." She said she had considerable experience in the field of consumer affairs during the 22
years she was in retailing.

Or if you study the full-page ads that list weekend specials
at various supermarkets, you might also come upon special
messages. For instance, there was this from the president of
the Grand Union Company, a chain with outlets in many
parts of the Northeast:

A CONSUMER BILL OF RIGHTS

We, at Grand Union, recognize that every consumer
has certain basic rights . . .

The Right to Know the things you want to know to
make informed, intelligent buying decisions—like more

complete price information, product freshness facts, and other kinds of product information.

The Right to Choice from a full line of brands—national and our own private label; from a variety of sizes and amounts to meet different family size needs; from products for every budget size; from products in different forms—fresh, frozen, canned, smoked and dried.

The Right to Satisfaction with every purchase. Or we will replace it without further charge, or refund the purchase price in full; or with a raincheck, if for any reason our store is temporarily out of an advertised special.

The Right to Be Heard in the president's office through postage paid letter forms available in every store and through your representative in management—our Director of Consumer Affairs.

But if someone in a later century were to discover a collection of clippings like these, would the impression the future reader receives accurately reflect present conditions? How much has the Consumer Revolution really accomplished?

As in so many other areas of public concern, the answers to these questions depend to a large extent on the point of view from which they are approached. Doubtless, Dr. Wiley would rub his eyes with amazement if he saw the massive new headquarters of the Food and Drug Administration, filled with highly trained specialists testing the fire resistance of fabrics and the poison content of paint used for children's toys, as well as the chemical properties of preservatives added to such products as "instant breakfasts."

But Dr. Wiley had the instincts of a born reformer, and

once he caught up with what had gone on during the past half century he would surely have mixed feelings. It is not too hard to predict that he would approve of many of the new protective programs, and speak their praise at every opportunity.

If a reporter had asked for his comment after the FDA told the American public to stop eating swordfish—because 90 per cent of the samples tested by the agency contained excessive amounts of mercury—Dr. Wiley almost certainly would have congratulated his successors. Bold moves like this, putting the mere possibility of harmful side effects above the profit-and-loss figures of any particular industry, always pleased him.

He would also have applauded the agency's new efforts to make unconcerned citizens realize some of the dangers facing them, for instance by printing large-type bulletins like *Your Money and Your Life: An FDA Catalog of Fakes and Swindles in the Health Field.*

Still, Dr. Wiley could hardly help agreeing with the criticisms of the new generation of crusaders. What if the agency did lack the money and manpower to do everything its critics wanted? That was a situation he knew all about, and he also knew how much pressure businessmen could exert. But neither of these seemingly constant problems could excuse the shameful weakness the FDA kept showing.

Why had the agency taken more than ten years to ban the additive known as MSG—or monosodium glutamate—from jars of baby food? The first laboratory evidence that this substance might cause brain damage should have brought an immediate ban, instead of a decade of hearings during which industry spokesmen calmly testified that mothers liked the way MSG improved the taste of strained meats and vegetables.

And why did so many questionable substances remain on the official "GRAS" list—the list of additives "generally regarded as safe," and therefore permitted in a large range of food products? No wonder so-called health-food stores were springing up everywhere, attracting increasing patronage with ads like:

A CHEMICAL THANKSGIVING?
Calcium propionate stuffing? Dried fruits with sulfur? Coal tar dyes in your salad oil? Stilbesterol in your eggs?

If you prefer a real Thanksgiving feast with real food, come to MAIN STREET GRAINERY . . .

Nevertheless, even Dr. Wiley would have to admit that the growing popularity of such natural food stores, not only in college towns and large cities but in practically every suburban community, was a hopeful sign. Where once only food faddists would think of patronizing such establishments, now even supermarket chains were finding it good business to provide at least a few shelves of unadulterated products.

Beyond the possible health benefits to the buyers of "pure" foods, this new awareness had a significance that Dr. Wiley would surely recognize. During his own crusading days, he had often felt rather lonely because so few people appeared to care about his efforts. Ralph Nader could scarcely have the same feeling when every mail delivery brings him more letters urging, "Keep up the good work!"

Politics had never been Dr. Wiley's strong point, but he would be bound to note that the great increase in public support for Nader-style consumerism had wrought some remarkable changes in the nation's capital. Of course, a lot of unfinished business remained—in his own special field of food and drugs, he could find many a legal loophole, not to mention a laxity of enforcement. And merely by reading the newspaper, he could see there was also much unfinished business in other areas of special consumer concern.

Poor workmanship. Shoddy materials. Planned obsolescence, where products were designed to be outdated, or even fall apart, soon after purchase. Repair service was still hard to obtain, and increasingly costly. "Buy Now, Pay Later" plans often contained unfair provisions. Trickery, and even outright fraud, were still far too common, especially among mail-order operators. Inferior or even dangerous products abounded, prices kept rising, and the poor consumer rarely could feel sure his or her best interests were not being undermined in some new manner.

Nevertheless, there were so many signs pointing in the opposite direction—toward the triumph of consumerism—that Dr. Wiley's spirits would probably not stay depressed. If he turned on a radio, he might hear an announcer's voice saying:

Mrs. Jones responded to an advertisement in a local newspaper concerning bathroom fixtures. The salesman who called at her home to estimate remodeling costs presented her with a more expensive plan after telling her that the advertised plan was inferior.

Mrs. Jones then signed a contract for an amount much higher than the price mentioned in the ad. She agreed to pay 24 monthly installments that included high interest charges which the contract did not explain.

Warning. Mrs. Jones was the victim of two deceptive business practices. First, she was "baited" into responding to an attractive advertisement and then was "switched" into buying higher-priced fixtures. Second, the hidden facts about the interest payments should have been disclosed according to the federal Truth-in-Lending Law.

Mrs. Jones should have been tipped off to the deceptive practices when the salesman was very reluctant to sell the advertised product. Reputable businesses advertise only what they intend to sell and will put the terms in writing.

To Dr. Wiley's mounting astonishment, the announcer might say that the preceding message was one in a continuing series taken from the files of the President's special assistant for consumer affairs. Similar commercials, courtesy of some local consumer group, were also appearing with increasing frequency.

Yet action would impress Dr. Wiley more than words. And if he spent a few hours going through the files of the Consumer Federation of America, for instance, he would not deny that a new attitude seemed to prevail among public officials. Instead of brushing aside consumer leaders as rather annoying but harmless, more and more political figures sought to prove themselves true friends of the consumer movement.

Forty-odd of the fifty states already had some special agency—usually part of their attorney generals' offices—which was supposed to defend consumer rights in the courts. Lawsuits aimed at recovering money lost through fraud were continuously being filed by these agencies, and in New York, where the first of these bureaus had been established, more than a million dollars a year was being returned to aggrieved buyers.

At the same time, in state after state, new "packages" of consumer protective laws were being passed by legislatures. Responding to increased pressure from organized consumers, some industrialized states were adopting stiffer rules than various federal agencies. For instance, Michigan had put into effect much stricter limits on the permitted contents of hot dogs than the United States Department of Agriculture had been willing to do. And in the highly complex area of regulating installment buying, several states were going further than the federal government to protect low-income consumers.

Yet the single most significant step was being taken in Washington. As early as the 1950's, Senator Kefauver had tried vainly to win support for a plan to set up a department charged with representing the nation's consumers. Just as the Department of Commerce served the business community, and the Department of Labor spoke for workers, and the Department of Agriculture helped farmers, the broad range of consumer interests would be the particular sphere of the new unit.

Under the original Kefauver plan, the many different consumer-protection programs already being administered by dozens of other agencies would all be concentrated in one department. Moreover, this department would also have the responsibility of defending consumer interests at every level of government policy-making.

But would combining the separate functions of enforcement and advocacy really work? Doubts about the wisdom of following the Kefauver plan had gradually increased. Did it actually make sense to propose such a massive reshuffling of government agencies? Even if some units of the Department of Agriculture and some divisions of regulatory agencies like the Federal Trade Commission could be brought into the same department as the Food and Drug Administration without causing severe bureaucratic headaches, would the change accomplish much in the long run? Experienced observers of the Washington scene thought not.

"Anytime you have an agency with the power to regulate

a particular industry, it's going to attract swarms of lobbyists pushing the industry's own point of view," one such observer noted. "The pressure is bound to have an effect. Sooner or later, the agency becomes too friendly toward the industry, and the public interest suffers."

Probably Ralph Nader's successes as an independent advocate of consumer interests had a great deal to do with the emergence of a different idea among many of the capital's decision-makers. If, without even having official status, Nader could achieve so much in the way of stronger consumer legislation, then why not set up an independent federal agency that might do the same sort of job still more effectively?

Thus, despite opposition from some consumer leaders who kept hoping for a grand new cabinet department, the process of arriving at a compromise plan began in earnest. It took patience and a willingness to face political obstacles of many kinds, but by the opening years of the 1970's, the outcome could hardly be doubted. To defend the interests of America's consumers, there soon would be a new arm of the federal government—the Consumer Protection Agency.

In 1970, the Senate passed a bill creating the CPA, but the House of Representatives failed to act on the measure. The following year, the House passed its own bill, and the Senate's Subcommittee on Government Operations opened hearings to resolve the differences between the two versions. Everybody familiar with the Washington political climate felt confident that the issue would soon be settled positively because President Nixon had already made it clear that he would sign a bill acceptable to both houses.

So the atmosphere in the hearing room provided a marked contrast to the tense and angry argument that had formerly accompanied congressional discussion of consumer protections. Compliments instead of complaints were the main order of the day.

"We've come a long way," commented Senator Charles Percy of Illinois, who had started his own career as an industrialist but was now supporting the proposed consumer "watchdog" agency energetically.

For it was generally agreed that the main role of CPA would be just that—a watchdog. When any agency of the government contemplated an action which might help or hurt the nation's consumers, the CPA would try to make other pressure groups realize that consumer rights had to be considered. At least, this was the objective of the new agency's supporters. Without the test of time, nobody could tell how effectively the CPA would work.

On one point there was no question—it would probably become one of the busiest offices in Washington. The range of proposed legislation having some consumer aspect had never been as wide as it was during these years when the Consumer Revolution reached what might be called its second stage. The long period of arousing public concern had ended, and this new era was marked by a different set of goals. Instead of seeking a base of support so that some fundamental reforms could be accomplished, consumer advocates now sought to follow through on the large backlog of unfinished business.

A regular monthly report on the current status of measures designed to improve consumer protections was put out by the executive branch of the federal government—a typical issue filled more than thirty pages. Among the topics covered were:

The setting of new federal standards for the warranties, or guarantees, that manufacturers gave to purchasers of their products.

The establishment of new federal safeguards to prevent fraud by mail-order houses.

The creation of new federal rules forbidding several common practices in the area of installment plans, notably the "holder in due course" doctrine still enforced by many states. Under this system, installment contracts could be sold by car dealers and other retail merchants to collection agencies that might legally prosecute even those buyers who withheld payments because their purchased items were defective.

The pamphlets also listed dozens of additions and amendments strengthening existing protections in such areas as auto safety and meat inspection. Consumer-education programs, new drug regulations, and a variety of measures under the general heading of environmental control received further attention, too.

Most consumer leaders were cautiously optimistic that all this activity would lead to lasting improvements. They had already seen too many instances where a new law had been timidly enforced to feel confident that progress could be taken for granted. But they had also seen so much evidence of widespread concern about consumer problems that they could not believe a new cycle of public indifference might erase the gains of the past decade.

What, then, did they think the future might hold?

15

Looking Forward

FOOD CANNERS PETITION FDA
FOR STIFFER REGULATION

A headline of the future? No, it actually appeared late in 1971 after a series of stories had come out about canned soups which had been improperly prepared and contained dangerous poisons. "We just don't think the canning industry can tolerate any more bad publicity," the head of the National Canners Association said, explaining why his group was appealing for help to the Food and Drug Administration. What the trade association wanted was no less than forty-eight pages of new regulations to tighten federal supervision over cannery processing, and thereby reassure the public.

Despite an incident like this, much of the public still felt government control intruded on freedom of choice. Reports describing a Federal Trade Commission hearing where a contingent of Nader's Raiders demanded an end to "wasteful" styling changes in automobiles prompted one irate citizen to write to *The New York Times:*

Sooner or later we must decide who is to run our lives
—ourselves, or self-appointed social theoreticians. . . .

To such a mentality, a car is transportation, clothing is insulation, food is fuel and protein, and so on. If there is no physiological need for chrome, vinyl upholstery, hot pants, eye shadow, garlic, cinnamon, flowers, or music, there is really no excuse for selling these things.

But back to the American automobile. Whether it meets the approval of Mr. Nader and his youthful entourage or not, it is a wonder of the world. And if we citizens want the chrome or the paint jobs changed from year to year, is it really so sinful?

May we not spend our own money as we wish?

At a Better Business Bureau meeting arranged to inform car dealers about the most common grievances among auto buyers, the dealers unexpectedly took over the program.

"How about some dealer protection?" one man shouted from his seat, and then launched into a bitter attack on "chiseling" consumers who kept trying to get more· than they had paid for.

A fellow dealer jumped up to condemn "instant experts" for telling the consumer he or she was being victimized when the truth of the matter was that the shoe was on the other foot. "The consumer doesn't just want satisfaction today," he said. "She wants vengeance!"

Although Better Business Bureau officials tried to get the meeting back to the official topic, they had little success in the face of repeated outbursts from the audience. "It's past midnight," one of the sponsors finally warned, "and unless these problems are dealt with constructively, they'll be dealt with in ways that may not benefit the industry."

However, the same kind of feeling was obviously bothering many businessmen. James M. Roche, the head of the

General Motors Corporation, put it more politely in a Chicago speech in which he said:

> Individuals and agencies have competed—sometimes blindly—to be on the crest of the wave of consumer protection. In the 1960's, consumer legislation came into political vogue. Much of this was necessary, and serves our society well. Yet the short-term political advantage offered by spectacular but unsound consumer legislation can do lasting damage to the very consumers it purports to help.
>
> The consumer is the loser when irresponsible criticism and ill-conceived legislation break down faith in our economic system, when harassment distracts us from our modern challenges, when the very idea of free enterprise is diminished in the eyes of the young people who must one day manage our businesses.

In short, the pendulum had swung quite far enough, and it was time to start leaving industry alone.

Even if this general point of view had wide appeal among the more conservative portions of the population, specific cases were likely to stimulate questions. For instance, the case of the defective engine mounts hardly helped Chairman Roche's cause. When the National Highway Traffic Safety Administration disclosed late in 1971 that eight million Chevrolets produced by General Motors between 1965 and 1969 had a construction weakness which could make the cars suddenly go out of control, another top GM executive insisted there was no reason for recalling all these vehicles to fix them. "A person driving a car should be a skilled driver," he said. "The condition takes place at very low speed where the car is completely controllable. It's no different than having a flat tire or a blowout where you don't expect it."

These words did not exactly reassure some drivers who wondered why the federal highway safety agency had not ordered the company to call back the cars. In fact, the government unit had no authority to do so. Under existing law, it could only issue warnings, and then if a lengthy inquiry demonstrated that a "potential risk" was actually a "safety defect," it could require the manufacturer to pass this information on to all buyers of the models affected. At that point, a company could recall the cars involved, and during recent years such recalls had become fairly common.

Still, the moral of the story about the engine mounts was plain to many consumers. Even after a decade of victories, their so-called revolution had not gone too far. Statistics reinforced this conviction. Figures compiled late in 1971 showed that only about 2.8 per cent of federal spending went for all the varied programs that were supposed to be informing, protecting, or otherwise benefiting consumers.

The leaders of the consumer movement hoped that the future would bring more than just additional funds to expand such programs. They also wanted new ideas to be adopted. Among their suggestions were:

1. The increased use of computers to store information for ready reference by consumer agencies.

2. The establishment of basic standards and grades to guide buyers.

3. The broadening of the legal rights of consumers, particularly in the direction of allowing group lawsuits which would make it easier to discourage unscrupulous manufacturers. Such "class action" cases could result in substantial fines instead of the much smaller penalties usually levied when a single aggrieved buyer sought court help.

Although efforts to achieve the last two of the above objectives had met strong—and largely successful—opposition in the past, consumer leaders were now somewhat optimistic about them partly because of the new branch of the legal profession personified by Ralph Nader—public-interest law. Although some people felt that one such advocate was one too many, and lawyers had no business departing from the old tradition of representing only specific clients, Nicholas Johnson, an outspoken member of the Federal Communications Commission, had a different estimate. "What the nation needs is a thousand Naders, not just one," he said.

And large numbers of college students were showing their agreement with Commissioner Johnson. Despite a decrease in the number of applications for many fields of advanced study, the nation's law schools had record numbers seeking admission at the beginning of the 1970's—more than they could possibly accept. These young men—and women, for more girls were applying than ever before—were generally among the brightest of their age group because the competition for admission was so stiff. They also tended to be among the most concerned with current problems. While some were motivated by the same desires for gaining a respected and comfortable place in society that had moved past generations of law students, others had a different reason for their choice of career. "If you think the system isn't working right, this is the best way to do something about it," a bearded senior who had started college with the intention of majoring in astronomy explained.

Thus it seemed increasingly likely that in years to come there would be more and more lawyers able and willing to play a Nader-style role in the consumer movement. Already many old and established law firms were discovering that, to attract talented young graduates, they had to consider certain new policies. Younger associates were often offered time and freedom to represent ghetto clients or practice some other variety of public-interest law. So the pressure for bringing legal codes into step with the changing times—to give as much attention to protecting the rights of consumers as the rights of producers—would almost surely keep mounting.

At the same time, too, there would probably be fewer occasions when a congressman could complain about "the empty chair." That was the phrase used by Representative Benjamin Rosenthal of New York, a veteran supporter of the consumer cause, when he talked about the one-sided cases frequently presented to lawmakers.

"How many times have we held a hearing where the lawyers for some special interest filled a whole table?" he would ask. "But if I wanted to hear from the other side—to hear about the consumer's interest in the matter—nobody took the witness chair. The empty chair represented consumers!"

Yet it was not merely from the ranks of the young that the growing army of public-interest lawyers might be recruited. In a television interview, Ralph Nader himself proposed another alternative. "There are a lot of retired people in this country who are lawyers and scientists and economists," he said. "They have a lot of experience, community contacts and the like, and they are getting tired of playing shuffleboard in Fort Lauderdale. Why not organize public-interest firms made up of professional retired people who will start all over the country? Seven, eight, twelve people in one firm becoming real activists, whether they're dealing with pension abuses or consumer fraud or inflation—any particular problem. Now that's what I think could be most effective."

However, it was undeniably the nation's youth who sparked another trend of special significance to the consumer movement. In effect, a good many young people have created a separate consumer revolution of their own by adopting a new set of values different from what they saw as that of their elders. "Buy! Buy! Buy!" The message that was constantly repeated by advertisers suddenly brought an unexpected response. "No! No! No!" First from college campuses, then from high schools, a mass refusal to wear what "the Establishment" decreed was the most obvious sign of the student revolt.

But blue jeans and T-shirts, instead of proper suits and skirts, were only one symbol of a much deeper change in attitude. Most older people, whether they viewed the youth movement with great alarm or saw it as a hopeful sign, soon realized this. Although only a militant minority of students went to the extent of outright violence to show their disgust with the way America was going, even the majority of their more peaceful classmates were obviously far from satisfied.

If the Vietnam war and racial injustice at home provided the fuel that fired the most explosive discontent, the same kind of issues consumer leaders had been raising for many decades inspired much of the calmer protest among students. Misleading labels, deceptive packaging, the failure of many business companies to put the public welfare above their own profits—these were the sort of symptoms the students seized on as evidence that "the system" was not working as it should. And perhaps because such things as the epidemic of drug abuse among young people struck many parents as far more dangerous, the consumer side of the campus unrest attracted more sympathy than might otherwise have been the case. "You can't *buy* happiness," sons and daughters kept telling their parents. Even parents who had never really examined their buying habits began to have second thoughts.

The result was that a dream—or nightmare—that had once seemed bound to come true no longer appeared to be imminent. Cherished as a dream by some advertising men and a nightmare by most consumer leaders, this vision pictured an America so absorbed with spending money that, in the heart of every city, people would keep filing endlessly through one vast supermarket, making purchase after purchase without any regard to need. And they never used what they bought more than a few times before throwing it away and buying a replacement.

By the beginning of the 1970's, such a vision seemed far away indeed. For there was a growing reluctance on the part of people of all ages to give in to somebody else's notion of what they ought to own.

How did industry react to this surge of antimaterialism? To it, this was only one of many new challenges. And, on at least two fronts, industry proceeded to prove something that its most thoughtful defenders had been saying all along—that it could adjust surprisingly easily to a different set of rules. In effect, industry stopped telling customers why a particular product was necessary, and let the customers tell it. Manufacturers became followers instead of leaders.

After insisting for many years that the American people really wanted only large and powerful cars, while the sales of small imported cars had gradually kept increasing, at last Detroit started putting out a full line of smaller economy models. Several of these turned into impressive money-makers.

Much more quickly and dramatically, a number of different industries found ways to profit from the changing tastes of many young people, as the *Wall Street Journal* soberly noted in a front-page story:

RICHES IN RAGS
_____

Companies Find Profits
In the 'Antimaterialism'
Of the Youth Culture
_____

Factory-Frayed Blue Jeans,
Invisible Makeup Products
Preserve a 'Natural' Look

The story went on to cite figures indicating that the nation's 8.2 million college students had $11.3 billion in available spending money every year. If all those under the age of twenty-five were included, their spending total rose to more than $40 billion. So the clothing and cosmetics industries had carefully adapted their output to appeal to young buyers, but the *Journal* noted that these canny manufacturers had not been the only businessmen to try the same policy:

> The counterculture's devotion to making things by hand has caused factories to produce an avalanche of products like leather goods, jewelry and pottery that look rough-hewn and hand-made but are actually mass-produced. . . . The entertainment industry and other communications media have latched on to the counterculture, too. Record producers and performers make fortunes on songs that echo, and sometimes inspire, anti-materialism—songs like "All You've Got Is Money," and "I Don't Want Your Cadillac."

Yet even if a portion of the American production machine was earning big profits by catering to special groups like the youth market, the basic challenge facing industry as a whole in this decade is much broader in scope. With a general downturn in the nation's economy, public officials, businessmen, consumer leaders, and ordinary citizens must face the question, How can continuing prosperity best be achieved?

Consumer leaders particularly had to keep in mind that if the ranks of jobless kept increasing and a severe depression should strike again, almost all else would fade into insignificance until the nation's economic health improved. Since the consumer movement by its very nature had a special interest in money matters, its supporters were probably more alert to the dangers of another great depression than were most people. Still, they could not help regarding the future from their own viewpoint. When the economic picture became increasingly cloudy, they put even more emphasis on consumer-education programs so that people who had less money to spend could do their spending as sensibly as possible. Consumer leaders also tried harder than ever to get the government to protect buyers who had to borrow money. But they could not agree with industry's argument that only a nation willing to keep up an endless spiral of buying things and more things could ever be free from the threat of hard times.

To consumer leaders, this continuing insistence on what they considered a harmful theory was just one more reason why businessmen as well as legislators desperately needed a new outlook. The rapidly growing concern about the environment was another, and the continuing pressure from minority groups seeking better treatment was still another. They gave this new outlook which rested on such a variety of grievances a rather unappealing name—corporate responsibility, and many considered corporate responsibility the most important domestic issue facing the United States in the 1970's. Students, professors, housewives—all put their hopes for America's future on the success of efforts to achieve reforms in this area.

What did corporate responsibility really mean?

For Ralph Nader, who had been largely responsible for focusing attention on this question, the definition had to start with a statistic. "Two hundred companies control almost 70 per cent of the country's manufacturing assets," he continuously pointed out, "and these companies have been increasingly utilizing or appropriating government resources or power." As examples of the way large industries were making their weight felt, he would cite case after case where government money or government grants of special privileges like mining licenses had been obtained without any regard for the public interest. Even more obvious instances of such disregard could be found in widespread practices of producing inferior goods and polluting the air or water with industrial wastes. According to Nader, the basic philosophy which allowed business to put profit-making above anything else had inevitably brought about an unhealthy situation in which corporations routinely behaved in ways that would be considered immoral if individuals behaved in the same manner.

"What's happened is that the corporation has received all the privileges under the U.S. Constitution of an individual without the responsibilities, and there's a tremendous gap operating here," Nader would insist.

It was to close this gap that groups of young lawyers and other specialists devoted to the consumer cause began campaigns during the early years of the decade. By electing consumer-minded people to corporation boards of directors, by revising some of the laws that let corporations escape severe penalty for antisocial actions, these relatively small but vocal groups hoped to achieve a far-reaching change in the fabric of American life.

"A society is in many ways like a fish—it rots from the head down," Nader contended. "Unless there's really an exemplary performance by people who've got the power, and got the privilege and the status, you can't expect a similar restraint on the part of people who have less."

Yet the scope of the Nader-inspired attack on corporate policies made many people besides business executives charge that the real motive of these so-called reformers was the destruction of America's system of free enterprise. Nevertheless, many new efforts by industry to show the public that it did care about the general welfare were started during the early 1970's. A number of corporations, ranging from airlines to telephone companies, appointed officials whose duty it was to serve as "watchdogs from within," guarding against policy that might conflict with the public interest. "Ombudsmen" with the similar function of being intermediaries between consumers and corporate executives were hired by other companies. Some major corporations expanded the membership of their boards to include representatives of minority groups.

Steps like these hardly satisfied consumer activists, who felt that more drastic moves were needed, but the increasing public discussion about what the role of the corporation should be in the complex world of the 1970's seemed an encouraging sign. After many years of mounting concern about a broad range of consumer problems, here was still another proof that the American people were no longer willing to accept the wisdom of the past as a sure guide to the future. Confronted by business practices that struck them as unfair or even dishonest, they were crying, "Enough!"

Already the revolt of the American consumer had brought great changes; in the second half of the twentieth century, this revolution had scored notable successes. And now, although it still had much unfinished business, there were good reasons for hoping that it might have an even stronger impact in the future.

Suggestions for Further Reading*

Since the Consumer Revolution is still happening, much of this book is based on interviews and on the recent files of leading newspapers and magazines. Readers who would like to pursue the subject further will find current periodicals their best source for up-to-date information. However, the following books may be helpful in providing additional background material:

Caplovitz, David, *The Poor Pay More*. New York: Free Press of Glencoe, 1963.

Carson, Rachel, *Silent Spring*. Boston: Houghton Mifflin, 1962.

Chase, Stuart, and F. J. Schlink, *Your Money's Worth*. New York: Macmillan, 1927.

Cox, Edward F., Robert C. Fellmuth, and John E. Schulz, *The Nader Report on the Federal Trade Commission*. New York: Baron, 1969.

---

* Large numbers of books, pamphlets, and other educational material about the consumer movement have been put out by various public and private agencies. Many of these are listed in the *Consumer Education Bibliography,* prepared under the direction of Mrs. Virginia Knauer, the President's Special Assistant for Consumer Affairs, in September of 1971. Copies of this 192-page publication, which describes films and filmstrips as well as printed materials, can be obtained for $1 from the Superintendent of Documents, U.S. Government Printing Office, Washington, D.C. 20402.

Graham, Frank, *Since Silent Spring.* Boston: Houghton Mifflin, 1970.

Kallet, Arthur, and F. J. Schlink, *100,000,000 Guinea Pigs.* New York: Vanguard, 1932.

Magnuson, Warren G., and Jean Carper, *The Dark Side of the Marketplace.* Englewood Cliffs, N.J.: Prentice-Hall, 1968.

Margolius, Sidney, *The Innocent Consumer vs. the Exploiters.* New York: Trident, 1967.

Masters, Dexter, *The Intelligent Buyer and the Telltale Seller.* New York: Knopf, 1966.

McClellan, Grant S., *The Consuming Public.* New York: Wilson, 1968.

Nader, Ralph, *Unsafe at Any Speed.* New York: Grossman, 1965.

Packard, Vance, *The Hidden Persuaders.* New York: McKay, 1957.

——, *The Waste Makers,* New York: McKay, 1960.

Turner, James S., *The Chemical Feast: The Ralph Nader Study Group Report on the Food and Drug Administration.* New York: Grossman, 1970.

Wiley, Harvey W., *An Autobiography.* Indianapolis: Bobbs-Merrill, 1930.

Young, James Harvey, *The Medical Messiahs: A Social History of Health Quackery in Twentieth-Century America.* Princeton: Princeton University Press, 1967.

Index

179

Index